Praise for *Your Playlist Can Change Your Life*

"Your mind is a powerful instrument. You are born with a melody in your brain, a song capable of keeping you balanced, bringing you peace from within and shaping your neurochemistry. *Your Playlist Can Change Your Life* will help you take charge, rewrite, replay, and make a difference in the rhythms that shape your life. *Your Playlist* shows you how to use your favorite songs to enhance your overall mental and physical performance. This book provides an easy and effective way to bring positive change into your everyday life."

—Sting

D0950994

YOUR
PLAYLIST
CAN CHANGE
YOUR LIFE

YOUR PLAYLIST CAN CHANGE YOUR LIFE

10
PROVEN WAYS
YOUR FAVORITE MUSIC
CAN REVOLUTIONIZE
YOUR HEALTH, MEMORY,
ORGANIZATION,
ALERTNESS, AND
MORE

GALINA MINDLIN, MD, PHD

DON DUROUSSEAU, MBA

JOSEPH CARDILLO, PHD

Published by Sourcebooks, Inc.
P.O. Box 4410, Naperville, Illinois 60567-4410
(630) 961-3900
Fax: (630) 961-2168
www.sourcebooks.com

Library of Congress Cataloging-in-Publication Data

Mindlin, Galina.
  Your playlist can change your life : ten proven ways your favorite music can revolutionize your health, memory, organization, alertness, and more / Galina Mindlin, Don DuRousseau, Joseph Cardillo.
    p. cm.
  Includes index.
  (pbk. : alk. paper) 1. Music–Psychological aspects. 2. Music–Physiological aspects. 3. Self-actualization (Psychology) I. DuRousseau, Don. II. Cardillo, Joseph, 1951- III. Title.
  ML3838.M647 2012
  781'.11–dc23
                              2011035363

Printed and bound in the United States of America.
VP 10 9 8 7 6 5 4 3 2 1

Dedications

For everyone with an open mind…
And for my family: husband, Denis; daughter, Alyona;
Mom and Dad; and my friends who are sharing
the passion and excitement with me in many
moments on my life journey.
—Galina

For my son, LCpl Gerald DuRousseau, USMC,
our military forces in harm's way, and to all our
nation's first responders, especially those who
assisted in my research.
—Don

For my wife, Elaine, and our daughters, Isabella
and Veronica, whom we loved before they were
born, and to my mother and father,
Josephine and Alfio Cardillo.
—Joseph

Without music, life would be a mistake.

—Friedrich Nietzsche

CONTENTS

ACKNOWLEDGMENTS

The authors wish to convey their gratitude to Linda Konner (their literary agent) and everyone at Sourcebooks, especially to Shana Drehs, Regan Fisher, Heather Hall, Katherine Faydash, Ashley Haag, Rachel Edwards, Danielle Trejo, Sarah Cardillo, Dawn Adams, Mallory Kaster, and Katie Casper.

Special thanks (from Galina) to BMT providers: Drs. George Rozelle, Orli Peter, Carol Kershaw, Bill Wade, Fred Kahan, David Mitnick, Susan Clear, Michael Cohen, Steven Kahan, Jane Price, Jim Evans, and all other providers.

Special thanks to her colleagues from Moscow Medical Academy: Professor Dr. Levin, who developed Brain Music, and his business partner, Dr. Goldstein; and to her BMT research team, Don DuRousseau, Dr. Deborah Haller, and Dr. Colette Haward.

Special thanks to her husband Dr. Kapkov and Dmitrij Gavrilov for providing BMT technical support and to her publicist, Janet Appel, who did an excellent job in raising public awareness of BMT, evidence-based technology. And special thanks to her colleagues who shared her enthusiasm for BMT and integrative medicine: Dr. John Slaughter and Dr. Richard Brown.

Special thanks to her parents, Rita and Eolf, who gave her an opportunity to graduate from music, dancing, and medical school and granted her the best of her "brain music." Special thanks to her daughter Alyona for embracing and inspiring her "brain music" and her husband Denis for sharing her music soundtracks with her in many ways.

Special thanks (from Don) to the National Sheriffs' Association and the International Association of Fire Chiefs for agreeing to participate in the brain music research, to Mary Margaret Walker for her dedicated efforts as a research assistant, and to Pamela DuRousseau, MPH, RD, for providing extensive knowledge of nutritional science related to development and long-term maintenance of brain health.

Special thanks (from Joseph) to his wife Elaine, daughters, and extended family and friends who supported him throughout this project; to the State University of New York for its many years of encouragement and support toward his research in whole-person health care; to his brother Alfred Cardillo for his guidance and deep expertise in health care; to all of his colleagues in holistic arts, sciences, and medicine; to his colleagues at *Psychology Today, Personal Excellence,* and *Smart Supervision* for encouraging his early writings on *Music On Your Mind*; and to his father, Alfio Cardillo, for sharing with him his love for music and especially for giving him his first violin lesson as a teenager.

INTRODUCTION

What could you learn about yourself if you could peer into your brain and see what it looks like when you are listening to your favorite music?

We all intuitively know how good it feels to get in our car, turn on the radio, and hear our all-time favorite song. But imagine being able to power up your brain with that clean, positive energy at will, anytime and anywhere, without negative side effects. Now imagine being able to think more clearly than usual, with a heightened perception of your surroundings, and being able to reach that state whenever you need to, wherever you are. It doesn't matter if your musical taste is Luciano Pavarotti, Bono, Billie Holiday, or Muse. You can achieve this state, and this book will show you how.

There is much new scientific research to document the profound influence of music on your physical, psychological, and spiritual well-being. In fact, whenever people come together for weddings, funerals, graduations, sports, worship, recreation, romance, dinner, or entertainment, music is there. Independent of our backgrounds and beliefs, our customs and traditions, music has a primary role in all aspects of our lives.

Historically, rhythm, music, and song have been used as a way to tune the mind, to heal the body, and to strengthen the spirit. Music is even viewed today as a way to connect to the universe itself. Not surprisingly, the core features of music are RHYTHM, HARMONY, RESONANCE, SYNCHRONY, and DISSONANCE (see glossary for definitions of terms), and those are the same processes the brain uses to coordinate its activities and carry out complex behaviors. This is why music can have such a profound effect on us.

Thanks to several new advances in neuroimaging technology, we now know that music affects every part of the brain and has the potential to exert powerful influence over its control systems. And because those systems regulate much of our thought processes and goal-directed actions, music can influence our perceptions, emotions, memories, neurochemistry, and ultimately our behavior. In the long term, music can begin to change how our higher brain systems operate by increasing our ability to adapt to stress and allowing us to evolve a new way of thinking, one in which you can use music as a support mechanism in all that you do.

Your Playlist Can Change Your Life is an attempt to take something we all already love—music—and view it through the lens of revolutionary, frontier neuroscience, which has opened a treasure chest of new and exciting ways to use the incredible elixir of music to enhance our daily lives.

Did you know that:

- The rhythms in the brain are organized by the same principles as music.

- Your brain processes music differently than language and mathematics, yet music can influence your proficiency in each.
- Musical processes that engage in the womb may affect you for the rest of your life.
- Calmness requires more of your body's energy than alertness, and music can help you set the balance between the two.
- Music, like scent, has an immediate neuro pathway that can bypass your thinking brain and directly affect your emotional state.
- Musical ability is natural to the human species and not just a rare talent.
- Your brain waves can be turned into musical notes using a computer and a mathematical algorithm, and that music can help improve your sleep, mood, and even on-the-job performance.

Most important, music can be used to trigger various mental states that range from being highly focused and vigilant to feeling an all-encompassing calm and relaxed attitude, all without having to use harmful drugs.

All you need to do is choose a playlist that activates the brain networks that will meet your demands and hit the play button. Your playlist will unlock your brain's hardwired musical remedy, ultimately putting you in your best mind-set to meet your goals. In short, you can use your self-prescribed personal playlist to achieve a higher level of mental functioning and to enhance your well-being in all that you do.

Based on many years of research as well as new research that is not available anywhere else, *Your Playlist Can Change*

Your Life will provide you with scientifically proven, step-by-step methods to use your favorite music to enhance your health, memory, organization, alertness, and more.

Today there is a burgeoning demand for personalized health care and wellness. People want information that is suited to them, solutions that are natural and effective. In this spirit, we're bringing our unique blend of expertise in NEUROPSYCHIATRY, NEUROPHYSIOLOGY, COGNITIVE NEUROSCIENCE, psychology, brain research, clinical medicine, and human performance improvement to bear in this book. We are on a mission, of sorts, to bring you a scientifically proven, self-regulatory program that uses one of life's greatest pleasures—music. Ultimately, you will get a glimpse of what goes on in your own brain when listening to your favorite playlist, and you will learn how to use the power of music to stay mentally sharp and focused, with increased rates of performance and with an enhanced ability to fight off stress, insomnia, anxiety, depression, and even addiction.

Your Playlist Can Change Your Life will take you to the frontiers of medicine, neuroscience, psychology, and personalized health care straight into a world of sound, rhythm, music, and song. It will unleash a seemingly magical force within your own brain that is capable of wielding great synergy within your body as well as your mind.

We speak as one voice in this book, but you're actually reading the combined experience and expertise of three people: Galina Mindlin, MD, PhD; Don DuRousseau, MBA; and Joseph Cardillo, PhD. You can read more about us on page 231, but we want to give you an idea of who your tour guides will be on this journey.

Galina is *Your Playlist*'s lead scientist. She is a founder of BRAIN MUSIC THERAPY (BMT) in the United States (you'll read more about BMT in chapter 10).

Don brings his unique blend of neuroscience and business expertise to *Your Playlist*. He is the founder and chief executive officer of Human Bionics, LLC, and the executive director of Peak Neurotraining Solutions Inc.

Joseph is a top-selling author in the fields of health, mind-body-spirit, and psychology. He has a doctorate in holistic psychology and mind-body medicine. He has taught at various universities, including the University at Albany and Hudson Valley Community College.

How to Use This Book

Each chapter presents one of ten scientifically proven ways that music can help you heighten your level of peak performance and achieve better health and harmony in your day-to-day living. You will learn how to:

1. Use songs to launch your brain into its most optimal mind-set
2. Use music to keep that mind-set flowing from one task to another, one day to another
3. Use music to bring calm to your daily routines and to train your brain to automatically start calming you whenever you need it
4. Use music to boost your mental alertness whenever and

wherever you need it and to train your brain to automatically spike your alertness when you need it

5. Use songs to intensify and train the release of feel-good, pleasure-producing neurochemicals to make you happier and to facilitate the successful achievement of many goals

6. Use songs to stimulate and train your brain into its best organizational mode and to transfer that mind-set to your daily activities

7. Use music to set your brain into its best remembering mode, to help you better commit anything to memory, deepen its storage, and recall it faster

8. Use songs to train your brain to get you into a mood, out of a mood, and through a mood, as well as to alter and enhance moods together with your partner; to overcome compulsive, addictive, and self-destructive behaviors; and to heal a broken heart

9. Use music to help you build bridges in your life to nurture your best potential and to help you live a freer, more creative, more authentic, and happier life

10. Use music to tap your ultimate soundtrack—the sound of your own brain waves—to enhance every aspect of your life (the sound of your brain waves can counter insomnia, anxiety, headaches, and attention-deficit/hyperactivity disorder, and they can boost your overall health, energy, alertness, creativity, and happiness)

We discuss in the pages of this book a wide variety of individuals who are using music to train their brains and enhance their lives. We intentionally focus on the usefulness and application of our research within the worlds of office workers, businesspeople, athletes, romantic partners, students, parents, the young, and the aging—you, all of us. *Your Playlist Can Change Your Life* is our attempt to home deliver frontier science to the widest possible audience so that we can all start benefiting from the great and beautiful life-enhancing powers of music.

Each chapter concludes with exercises intended to help you apply its concepts and techniques in a wide variety of life situations. To experience the full benefit of these activities, repetition and practice—which is the hallmark of any good training regimen—are necessary. Thus, the more often you practice, the more automatic and powerful the effects of both the exercises and the music will be.

Because no two people's experiences are exactly alike and each person's needs and tastes differ, we have designed the exercises to help you personalize your own playlist to match your individual goals. Feel free to adapt or modify either of them at any time. Experiment—and most of all have fun.

Your Playlist Can Change Your Life is not a guidebook—it is designed to be read and applied at your own pace. You can move slowly through its pages, allowing yourself time to absorb the many techniques that each chapter offers. You can also read through quickly and then return to those chapters most appropriate to your current life situations. Most information in this book is easy to absorb. But again, the concepts and techniques here require practice as you experience different pieces and types of music and glean for yourself the most benefit from a particular playlist.

For your convenience, we have included a glossary of musical and scientific terminology. Terms that are bolded in the text are included in the glossary.

The process of learning to nurture ourselves with music is a riveting one. If used successfully, *Your Playlist Can Change Your Life* will help you cleanse your mind of negative and unwanted thoughts and emotions, thus making it easier for you to reach personal goals, to maintain alertness, or to achieve an all-encompassing calm. You will think more clearly. You will feel more relaxed. You will enjoy greater mind-body synchronicity and feel more tuned to your goals. And you will gain more confidence in your ability to achieve personal wellness. Many amazing things will likely occur. May the concepts and techniques described within these pages serve you well; they have for each of us!

Chapter 1

HOW TO USE MUSIC TO MAKE YOUR MIND FLOW

Music is what life sounds like.

—Eric Olson

Imagine your mind uncluttered, happy, and free. For most of us, that's not a reality. But we used to have a mind like that. At birth, a free-flowing, feel-good mind is as natural to all of us as breathing. Mihaly Csikszentmihalyi, in his seminal book *Flow,* defines that kind of FLOW as "a state of concentration so focused that it amounts to absolute absorption in an activity." Research shows that we naturally operate in a flow mind-set up to about the age of five, when it usually begins to wane.

But the good news is that we can regain flow at any age. Imagine having that mind-set—fresh and unfettered, fast and clean—in almost an instant, helping you vault into your best performance to meet your goals. Whether you need to bolster your alertness because you are a little too mellow for a task, calm yourself down because you are too much on edge, strengthen your memory, rein in your emotions, increase your organization, boost your immune system, or just amplify your enjoyment of life, flow can help you reach these goals.

One of the best ways to achieve this flow is through music, because music has been with us since the beginning.

The Music Deep in Your Cells

Your mind-body connection to music is nothing less than dazzling. In fact, the first music encoded deep within your memory are the earliest vibrations that made you—the rhythms and tempos of your first cells. Imagine this: as your cells began to develop with the comforting rhythms of your mother's heartbeat and the whooshing, low-frequency sounds vibrating through her placenta and your umbilical cord, these first musical scores began ENTRAINING (two or more rhythms synchronizing into one) in your brain and orchestrating the essence of music for your entire being. So from your first sparks of life, your brain was already establishing the relationship for how music affects you today.

But can you remember these early musical memories? Newborns can almost immediately show some memory of sounds they encountered in the womb. Although babies react to only about one-third of all surrounding available sounds within the first six hours of birth, they begin to react more and more as the weeks progress. Before any of us is capable of speaking words, we can recognize changes in notes and rhythmic patterns. What's more, researchers have demonstrated that if you play a piece of music repeatedly to a child before birth, and then play the same piece within a month after birth, the child is able to recognize it. And we know that soon after birth, infants can instantly respond to their mom's soothing voice singing a lullaby, especially if they were exposed to the song during the last three months of pregnancy. These kinds of musical memories can help you get your mind FLOWING for your entire life.

During your first six months of life, you learn to make meaning out of what you hear. Throughout all this development, lyrical and comforting MOTHERESE—the singsong ways in which parents speak to their children before and after birth—plays a significant role in instilling feelings of calm, safety, and love. (Motherese sounds the same no matter what language you speak or historical time frame you consider; the effect is the same.) When you imagine a mother cradling her baby in her arms, speaking gently and sweetly, the two are psychologically and physiologically wrapped in a feeling that zooms through time and space, from mother to child, a feeling that has endured for millennia. In a way, it is not surprising that only by their fourteenth week, children can distinguish their own mother's footsteps from anyone else's and discriminate between their mother's voice and a stranger's.

These early musical influences stay with us for our entire lives. It's no wonder that you can go to the beach on any given day and see a man or woman lying in the sand, eyes gently closed, listening to the whoosh of waves and the easy hush of wind, smiling like a baby, not really knowing why it all feels so good, just loving it, flowing with it, comfortably and calmly. It's as though nature has planted a computer chip in our emotional brain that triggers deep, primitive pleasure at the slightest echo of the sounds that were there during your making. This is literally the flowing music of your own, personal lullaby—sounds so powerful that, years later, they can short-circuit negative thoughts in just milliseconds or reroute a day headed for catastrophe into one headed for victory.

We'll talk more later in this chapter and later chapters about how to start putting your playlists together, but throughout the book you'll find tips and ideas like this one: you might consider including in your playlists some of the sounds associated with your own primitive melodies, the ones you were listening to while you were in your mother's womb. Water sounds, breezes, heartbeats, and other environmental sounds and songs are examples of this. These will help you achieve flow, ramp up an experience, and sustain it.

Consider this: when a woman is pregnant, she is especially aware of what sounds and sound combinations make her irritable (e.g., a dog's incessant barking, a siren, specific words), and she is unconsciously protective of her baby, restricting the baby's exposure to those sounds. The same sounds that affected our mothers can also make us irritable—or on the flip side, the sounds that made her happy can make us feel relaxed and happy. For this reason, many cultures have encouraged expecting mothers to listen to soothing music during their pregnancies. By doing so, they not only protect their children in the womb but also give them a solid way— music—to optimize their mind-set as they grow older.

This genetic component is real and very important. Just like medications, various sounds and musical pieces are more effective for us if they have had a positive effect on one of our parents. If you have a close relationship with your mother, you have a great opportunity to explore the songs and sounds your mom was listening to before you were conceived and especially during the time you were in her womb. For example, what made her feel relaxed or alert or happy? What made her mind flow? Listen to those sounds and songs for yourself. If they work well for you, add them to your playlist. Listen to them whenever you want the specific effect they enhance.

One of Dr. Mindlin's patients tells this story about how she learned to tap into sounds that affected both her mother and grandmother. She now uses them to launch her into a flow state whenever she needs to get there: "I had just entered—more exact, ran—into my office building, where I was about to hold an important meeting in ten minutes. I needed to get my mind into the zone, so to speak, and flowing. But my head was spinning a hundred miles an hour. So I reached for my iPod and cued up "Waterfall" [the sounds of a waterfall in nature]. This usually works for me almost flawlessly, and it worked here."

She continues: "The first time I discovered this calming effect was years ago when I was visiting my grandmother in Canada. She lives, and always has, near Niagara Falls. My family history in a way is steeped in the sound of the falls. My grandma would sit along the falls and let the sound of all that powerful water put her mind in a sweet place for hours while she was pregnant with my mom and then my mom quite often did the same with me. Even though my family moved to the United States when I was two, and I barely remember

Niagara Falls on that visit to grandma's years ago, the sound still has an instantaneous calming effect on me. Now this is my prescription for taking the edge off and getting into my best mental zone."

So music—in perhaps its most primordial form—links our brain to vibrations we experienced as babies that have both long- and short-term effects on our brain's circuitry. In the coming pages, we will see how the core characteristics of music—RHYTHM, HARMONY, SYNCHRONY, RESONANCE, and DISSONANCE can affect frequencies in our brain and extend their influence on our hormones, neurotransmitters, and essential enzymes, and can ultimately affect our focus, feelings, moods, motivations, organizational power, and even pleasures.

Like infants cooing in their mother's arms, with no cares in the world, it is possible for us to go through a day at work feeling that same special way. All we need is to find the music that keeps our mind on track.

> ▶▶ I remember my childhood in the North Pole, where I was born. All those white nights have remained in my brain with the sound of "white noise," almost like a silent music of eternity.
>
> My state of calm was influenced by this eternity of white music and nights, which created, for me, a powerful silence. So now I often turn off all the sounds in my brain, even if just for a minute, to bring me back to my calm state and to achieve my maximum focus. Then I go to my playlist and pick the best music to enhance whatever task I am about to pursue.
>
> —Galina

Music Is User Friendly

Next to the sense of smell, music is the fastest, most user-friendly way to influence and reset your brain networks without using an external substance or drug. The effects are virtually immediate.

Here is how it works: When you listen to and perceive music, blood flow and oxygen increase in different areas of the brain. Sound transmitted to the inner ear is broken down into a wide spectrum of frequencies. Individual nerve cells transmit messages about each sound and its nuances from the inner ear into small nuclei clusters deeper in the brain. As other areas of the brain repeat this and process it, exciting and quelling the many systems differently, the brain generates the feelings, thoughts, and memories that you experience when listening to a particular piece of music.

And as we have said, the effects can be powerful both in intensity and in the changes they trigger. For example, in just a millisecond, music can change patterns in your brain waves, which are electrical currents in your brain.

Music Changes Brain Waves

We measure brain waves by using an ELECTROENCEPHALOGRAPH (EEG), which picks up the frequency of brain waves through electrodes placed on the scalp. From highest to lowest these frequencies are called BETA, ALPHA, THETA, and DELTA.

Beta is your waking state, the one in which you feel most alert.

Alpha waves are slower. They make you feel relaxed,

reflective. Alpha waves engender a state of mind often associated with meditation, a relaxed alertness.

Theta waves are even slower. They can be associated with deeper relaxation, the state of mind you feel between wakefulness and sleep. Theta is sometimes referred to as dreamer's brain.

Delta is the lowest frequency. This is the state of mind in which deep sleep occurs. It is also associated with trances.

What do these frequencies have to do with your playlist? By changing certain frequencies in your music, you can move through a variety of mental states that range from high alert to fully relaxed. That means that you can use your playlist to move from an alert mind-set into a meditative, more relaxed state, or even into the drowsy, dreamy range—and vice versa. And you can make those changes last.

Music Changes Brain Wiring

Imagine entering your next office meeting or going about any important daily task and feeling your mental best, simply by listening to a favorite tune. Possible? Absolutely!

Your brain's PLASTICITY (ability to change at any age) helps you create long-term change and even target those changes to specific tasks and goals. We're all familiar with learning new motor skills to perform certain physical activities. Say, for example, that you learn a new tennis serve. Your brain lays down new wiring to enable you to perform it.

Likewise, if you play a song over and over during a specific situation—say you are stuck in traffic and play a tune from your playlist that you know calms you—you can train (and rewire) your brain to automatically send your mind and body new instructions on how to relax you whenever you are stuck in traffic. Your brain's plasticity makes this change possible.

The song can be anything you like—what's important is that you know that it will give you the effect you desire. One person's choice may be "You've Got a Friend" by James Taylor or Jewel's "You Were Meant for Me"; another's may be "Wonderful Tonight" by Eric Clapton or Johann Pachelbel's Canon.

Playlist Bonus

To really pump up the effect that music has on rewiring your brain, first play a song or recording of a natural sound, such as a waterfall, that for you turns off all the other sounds in your brain and sends you into that luxurious state of flow that you knew as a child. Then play that certain song that really works for you—you'll see the effects amped up.

Researchers say that in about three weeks' time, with as little as two five-minute applications from your playlist a day, you can change a behavior—you can go from feeling frenzied as you drive through traffic to feeling relaxed and flowing instead. Again, any kind of music will do the trick. It doesn't matter if you're listening to Mozart, Bono, or a recording of a waterfall.

Keep on the Flow

Music makes it easy to get into a state of flow and to sustain it, because music is already programmed into your brain's wiring. Professional musicians, for example, commonly experience this mind-set. Some of the iconic jam bands come to mind, bands like Cream, the Grateful Dead, the Allman Brothers, and Crosby, Stills, Nash, and Young. Just pick one of these or any group you like and imagine both the individual musicians and their respective band members playing, getting into a groove, matching one another on their instruments note per note, chop per chop, until they crescendo into a massive tidal wave of great sound. When you see such performances live, the whole audience gets into the flow of it all as well, which becomes synergistic—looping from one person to the other, then throughout the whole crowd, then back to the performers, who in turn feed it back to the crowd and so on until everyone is completely absorbed into the activity.

> ▶▶ A friend and colleague involved in years of laboratory research in microbiology used to clear out his head and drive his brain into a flow state first thing upon entering his lab. It became a daily ritual. His choice of music was always classical and his favorite tunes were fast piano pieces like Mozart's Sonata in C Major. Once he was in his zone, he would turn his attention to research. He began this ritual while working on his doctorate and has never stopped.
> —Joseph

The elements of rhythm, harmony, resonance, synchrony,

and dissonance—core elements of both music and brain activity—help make this loop possible and sustain it. Interestingly, your brain uses these same elements to coordinate its own activities and communicate intentions throughout its many SUB-NETWORKS. Here's what we mean.

Rhythm is a pattern or recurrence of beat. It refers to the duration of notes in a series and the way they group together. For example, in the Jackson 5 song "ABC," the lyrics, "A, B, C," and "1, 2, 3" and "Do, re, mi" are all equal in duration.

Rhythm is involved in many brain areas and often allows us to do things without any thinking. It is particularly involved in areas of the brain that support our sense of timing, sequencing, speech, and movement. In addition, our ability to remember rhythms is nothing short of remarkable. Most people can sing a song from memory in virtually the same rhythm they last heard it performed. They can also easily detect when something is off, like when an extra beat has been added. You hear "Baa-Baa Black Sheep," and even though you haven't heard it in years, you have a sense that it is right, whereas if you heard "Baa-Baa-Baa Black Sheep," you would instantly sense that it was incorrect. So the brain is able to store and recall rhythmic settings. And we use this capacity for many things—like dancing, jogging, swinging a baseball bat, speaking, writing, processing and responding to information, calming, becoming alert, and so on.

Harmony is a parallel melody—a cluster of notes played or sung simultaneously to the original or main melody. The Everly Brothers; the Beach Boys; the Temptations; Simon and Garfunkel; Crosby, Stills, Nash, and Young; and the B-52s have been known for their unique harmonies. Through subtle differences in connections within and across its hemispheres, the brain uses harmony to make sense of incoming information, to plan responses, and to take actions.

Synchrony refers to all of the parts of a musical composition staying on beat or in step, and it typically requires a leader or conductor to keep all the parts working together. In the brain, the frontal cortex, which monitors all of the brain's activity, sends directions back through connections in both halves of the brain to keep everything coordinated.

Resonance is the duration of a note, its reverberation. This echoing sense can add drama—say, the difference between someone singing or playing an instrument in a large concert hall or long, high stairwell and someone performing in a small office space. The song "With or Without You" by U2 provides a great example of both instrumental and vocal resonance. Resonance in the brain coordinates and maintains control of many activities. It is the feedback that must occur to prevent certain activities from running wildly out of control (e.g., seizure) or shutting off completely (e.g., coma). So resonance (feedback) signals when something has gone wrong and allows the brain to communicate information that will coordinate and restabilize its activities.

Dissonance refers to unpleasant-sounding chords and intervals; pleasing ones are referred to as consonance. Musical harmonies or beats that seem distant or slightly incomplete, and that your mind wants to correct or resolve, are examples of dissonance. And when in a musical composition they do strategically resolve themselves, they can evoke great pleasure when it all comes together.

Examples of dissonance are the feigned, elongated endings to songs that many groups use to drive audiences wild, especially at rock concerts. Everybody loves these. Bands set up expectations and boost tensions by making you think that the song is going to end with each and every beat—but you have to wait for that final chop to come down before it actually does. A classic example of this is the Who's "Won't Get Fooled Again," with Pete Townsend's gigantically fat guitar chords driving through the synthesizer interlude until Roger Daltrey's voice finally sails through the whole wall of sound and brings resolution to the piece.

Another good example of dissonance is the Mamas and the Papas song "I Saw Her Again Last Night," with the famous "extra" three words right before the chorus: "I saw her / I saw her again last night"—the result of vocalists coming in one bar too early. The mistake, however, landed this song a place in rock-and-roll history when producers decided to keep the "error" in the final cut. The extra words added a momentary incompleteness and expectation that resolved so perfectly when the whole band came in at the right time that anyone listening would think it intentional.

Dissonance in the brain is likely the most important characteristic in how your brain carries out communication and behaviors. Dissonance is how the brain indicates that something is different, that a mismatch has occurred and that something in our environment has changed and must be dealt with. This starts a cascade of neurochemical events needed to get you to the peak of excitement while remaining still emotionally stable. For instance, if our ancestors were sitting in a clearing eating a meal and a lion jumped out of the grass, something would have to change—very quickly. Those whose brains responded fast enough to make the right choice of where to run were rewarded with survival. Those who froze in panic and fright were likely eaten. It's through dealing effectively with dissonance that the lucky ones were able to escape and live on to the next encounter. Dissonance is at the core of how the brain rapidly communicates with all of its systems at once to make your body leap into action.

Your brain can recognize the elements of rhythm, harmony, resonance, synchrony, and dissonance (in music and in other sound) and use them to achieve its overall best performance while generating deep feelings of pleasure and reward. Your brain can use those elements to get into flow.

> ▸▸ A student of mine recently told me a story about how her mother always played certain traditional songs while the two of them worked around the house when she was younger. The songs, according to her, always helped put them in a good mood and flow through chores. Now years later, she says with a smile, "I always play the exact same songs and in Spanish, just like my mother did. I can't do work around the house unless I play them. They organize me and make me happy. They make everything a breeze."
> —Joseph

Having this free-flowing, feel-good mind-set is important because, once you enter it, you can transfer it to other tasks and goals. This optimized flow mind-set is the basis for facilitating all other skills presented in this book, as it helps you combine those skills to establish relationships that will take each skill to higher levels of effectiveness.

For example, seeing the relationship among using music to become alert, using musical memories to energize your focus, and using the emotions that music triggers to deepen your storage of information can all help you pack a wallop at the next business meeting, public speaking engagement, or on your next test. Whatever the task, whatever your goal with regard to the skills and techniques you'll find in this book, a flowing mind will maximize your performance.

Putting Together Your Playlist

Here is how to begin choosing songs for a playlist that will help you get into and sustain flow.

▸ **First, pick songs that you like a lot.** This is the most important thing. When you like a song, it activates brain networks and functions that will amplify and sustain whichever of the effects in this book you are working toward.

▸ **Pay attention to when a certain song works and when it doesn't.** For example, a piece like Tchaikovsky's *The Nutcracker* may put your mind in a state of flow on the way home from a long day at work because you and your family have enjoyed it performed many times and it brings on a cascade of happy, exhilarating thoughts. It is possible that the piece feels great to you on the way home but not very great on your way into work in the morning, when it leaves you feeling irritable.

▸ **Ingrain songs into your memory.** Once you have a song that works at a certain place and time (it puts you into a flow mind-set precisely when you want), start using it then. Play it when you are in the targeted situation and play it several times to start ingraining it into your memory. This step will help make effects like entering flow (and all the others) automatic—that is, your brain will start to enter flow (or one of the other effects) as it recognizes the targeted situation (e.g., your day is over and you are heading home). This is why, after just a few days of training, you can already hear the song playing in your head before you even turn on your iPod, MP3 player, or CD player. Your brain is already going right where you want it to.

▸ **Make a playlist that is task oriented.** For example, assemble a playlist titled "Driving Home." Start with the song or musical piece that you know works (e.g., *The Nutcracker*) and then experiment, adding others you think may work, removing them if they prove ineffective and allowing yourself to substitute others (or add others) later. Any additions should enhance the specific effect you want (e.g., flow, deep calmness, alertness) and make you feel more of that effect.

▸ **Train your brain with your assembled playlist.** This means train your brain like you would your muscles in a gym. You need to be relentless and train often. Play your song over and over and specifically within or in very close proximity to the exact time and situation you are trying to enhance with your playlist—like the scientist clearing his head with Mozart first thing upon entering his lab, every day. Train like this relentlessly until your brain gets the message and creates new wiring to begin automatically sending instructions to your mind and body that you want this (specific) behavior whenever you are in your targeted situation.

▸ **Make a variety of playlists that target different situations.** Some suggested playlists are "Driving to Work," "Driving Home," "Energizing Lunch Break," "Going to Meetings," "Before Tests," "Before Speaking to the Boss," "Driving to Pick Up My Date." You may find that your "Driving to Work" choices are also great for your "Energizing Lunch Break" or other situations in which you need a pick-me-up. Go for it—add them to those lists too. You may even find that you only need one of the tracks for certain situations and that you like repeating it. All of this works. Nothing works better than customizing your playlists to suit your own mind and body and needs.

▸ **Arc your playlist.** As you use your playlist for a specific situation, you will eventually want to arc it (assuming you are using more than one song). This can be done in various ways—organizing from slower to faster, from soft to loud, or from less emotional to more emotional. You can build your tracks up to a climax, or you can sequence them so that after they peak, they slowly or quickly work their way back down. The choice is yours. The benefit to arcing is that it will help you better sustain your mind-set.

For example, a certain individual may like to start his drive home with "Christmas Song" from *The Nutcracker*, but after that need something that can energize him a little more to get his mind flowing. So he puts on Steve Winwood's "Higher Love" followed by the Rolling Stones' "Brown Sugar" (which is right when traffic predictably starts getting heavy) and that's exactly when he wants to hear Bruce Springsteen's "Born to Run"—which he can count on to launch him into the state of flow he is looking for. So, he repeats it several times to keep him there until he gets to the last stretch of highway home, which is exactly where "Small Town" by John Mellencamp comes on, igniting memories for him of where he grew up as a kid, a small town in New York's Catskill Mountains. And if he can time it just right, he can hear the Byrds' version of "Chimes of Freedom," which seals the deal as he pulls into his driveway flowing and happy.

We talked about "tricking" your brain in the introduction—using the techniques in this book to significantly boost the natural effects music already has on your life. In the forthcoming chapters, you will learn many more techniques to help you use the music you love to facilitate your daily goals in ways that are new to you. These concepts and skills will build on one another incrementally so that by the end of the book, your ability to design playlists to self-regulate your mind and body will become amazingly sharp and accurate. You will learn how to associate multiple brain areas when you listen to your songs and how turning on these areas amps up music's ability to train your brain to operate at its peak performance, like the phenomenal instrument it is. At the end of each chapter, we will continue our recommendations in "Putting Together Your Playlist," adding that chapter's techniques to your list of to-dos." With this in mind, we recommend that you read through each chapter sequentially at first and then return to those sections that most apply to your current daily needs.

Exercise

1. **Use Natural Sound.** Everyone—adults, teens, children, and families—can enjoy this exercise and tap some of our deepest and earliest musical memories. Find a quiet place. At first, pick a spot where you can find natural sounds that we all find relaxing, such as a quiet area near a stream or a park. Sit and relax. Breathe slowly—inhale through your nose and exhale through your mouth. Use the bottom of your lungs to pull the air in. Try focusing on slowing your breathing to six or eight deep breaths per minute. This will help you reduce your level of psychological stress and feel more refreshed. You can even try to make the sound you're listening to yourself a few times. This will help give your brain the idea that the information is important and ingrain it into your memory. Listen to yourself mimicking the sound. Overall, just listen closely. If there is water near, listen to the nuances of its sound. Relax and try to keep your attention on the sounds. Do this for five to ten minutes or for however long feels comfortable. With practice, try to work your way up to twenty minutes. Revisit this exercise often.

   Try finding a download that is similar to the sound and add it to your playlist. Use it as is or in combination with other recordings (as prescribed in this chapter) to help you enter and sustain flow.

Chapter 2

HOW TO USE MUSIC TO KEEP YOUR MIND FLOWING

The pause is as important as the note.

—Truman Fisher

Most athletes have had someone say to them at one point or another, "Stop what you are doing and just take a minute to breathe." They have also heard the opposite, "Come on, let's go, go, go!" Coaches say things like this because they have seen time and again the cost of players losing their flow because they have become too wired or, the opposite, too lackadaisical. Either state can derail an athlete's performance. There is a delicate mental balancing act all of us—not just athletes—must learn if we want to get into our optimum mind-set and sustain it.

Working in the kitchen provides a good example of balance. You may have seen shows like *Iron Chef America* on television, where some of the best chefs in the country compete against one another to see who can prepare the best meal from surprise ingredients, in a very short time. The chefs usually put on an impressive show of talent while staying calm and focused and getting their creative and often complex dishes prepared. What a lesson in balance. You can see their highly energized focus as they move from one task to another with calm grace and optimum precision, which flows right to the end, when time is running out, and they lightly place that one last "something" on their dishes to give them that perfect finishing touch.

Losing your own flow in a competition, athletic, culinary, or otherwise, can be catastrophic, as it can also sometimes be in daily life.

If you have ever had to take a test or give a speech and, at the last minute, had someone tell you that your starting time has been delayed, then you know all too well what it feels like to have your energy unplugged, so to speak. You know, at that point, that you will have to work your way back into the flow of things if you are going to give it your best. And doing this relies on your ability to balance as well.

In the neurophysiological sense, you are balanced when your mind is operating in a middle ground between an activated (focused and energized) state and a relaxed (calm) state. This balance allows you to function at your best. By middle ground, however, we do not mean that you are only partially calm and partially focused—far from it. We mean that you are optimally calm and optimally focused. The point is that if you increased either your calm or your focus any more, your overall performance would begin to deteriorate.

Having the right balance of each allows you to proceed with whatever your current task is in a state that's both calm and simultaneously highly focused. This allows you to hit your optimum performance because you are flowing and functioning at your best.

Think of it like this: Imagine having made the perfect cup of coffee (perfect temperature and perfect flavor) and wanting to keep it that way—at its optimum—until you are finished drinking it. The coffee gets cold. So you put it in the microwave, but when you take it out, it is a little too hot, so you add cream. Now it is too cool, so you warm it again. It comes out slightly too hot and the flavor is a little thin, so you balance it off with a dab more coffee, and adjust it until it is optimum again.

Similarly, for your brain to reach its optimum performance, it has to make adjustments. It has to balance between turning on just the right amount of activity in one area (the part that keeps your mind aroused and focused) and just the right amount in another area (the part that keeps your mind calm). Your brain's frontal lobes are the control center, managing all of this to get you the best mix.

Your brain organizes itself into either a calm or a focused state by changing your brain waves, making them run more slowly or more quickly. This in turn makes you feel either calmer or more focused.

Let's revisit brain waves to get a better picture of what's happening. Delta waves, for example, move from one to four pulses per second; theta pulses at five to eight times per second; alpha at eight to twelve; beta at thirteen to thirty; and gamma waves (higher than high beta) at more than thirty per second. As we said previously, alpha and theta waves are associated with a state of calm, and beta waves catapult you into a focused state of mind.

When you are doing a math problem, for example, your alpha and theta waves go down, and your beta waves go up. Your frontal lobes manage the mix of brain waves so that you are able to adjust your state of calm or focus as either begins to wax or wane too much. This process helps you stay in the flow of things and keeps you operating at your optimum.

This is where your playlist comes in. With the right music it becomes possible to send your brain waves up or down and into your optimal mind-set.

Resetting Your Brain Waves to Optimum

This section provides two examples to show how different individuals used their playlists to help move themselves into a balanced mind-set for two very different goals. The first is from a college student who was trying to get his mind into its best gear for taking a final exam. The second is from a young woman, a library assistant, trying to get her mind in shape after a close encounter the night before a big meeting.

Our college student is standing at the front door with his headphones on, about to leave the house to take a final exam. He's trying hard to focus on the music. All he wants to do is get out of the house in his best frame of mind and avoid anything that could have an opposite effect. Before he can get out the door, he hears his mother's loud voice, complaining to his dad:

"Look at him! Instead of looking at books, he's got those earphones on!"

Then his dad cuts in. "Leave him alone," he says. "It's too late anyway; the test is today."

"That's exactly what I am saying," his mother says. "Today he needs time to get focused beforehand, not listen to his stupid iPhone. I don't see the logic."

But that's how he does it. As usual, to get himself in a calm mind state, he starts with his favorite electronic music. It's not for everybody, but for his restless brain, it puts him in the right frame of mind, a working one. His music mix starts out with an ultracool, modern electronic group, Pretty Lights. The first song is a relaxing track called "Finally Moving." He follows this with a fast-paced tune of theirs called "Keep Em Bouncin," which he cranks up considerably louder. He follows that with something even louder, DJ Tiësto's "Power Mix" and the synthesizer, electric violin, and percussion sounds start pushing his alertness toward the max. Then he has a couple of minutes of techno, like "Fly High," which is more monotone but creates just the right rhythm for him. This works like a fast metronome, synching his brain to the pace he wants and putting him right where he needs it.

And now our library assistant. It's the day before she has scheduled an appointment with her boss to initiate a discussion about getting a raise. She has been working at her job for about a year. She feels that she has really put in her time, too—doing a lot of good work and connecting well with both patrons and other employees. She knows she is overqualified for the position she holds and that she does equal work to others in the same position but does not make as much money as they do. She knows that some have been there longer than she has, and so she is not expecting to make more than them—just more than she is currently making. She also could use the extra pay.

She is already a little nervous about how her meeting will go. It's true that some people she knows use, let's say, extra stuff to help them get over their nerves, but to be honest, all she uses is a little music. In fact, she's been "using" for about two months. Specifically, she uses an old, Russian country song that her grandma would hum to herself while serving big family dinners. She loved hearing that song as a child—and still does—and loved hearing her grandmother hum it. When she has gotten herself into situations where she is feeling jumpy, she thinks about the melody and lyrics as a way to give herself a sense of strength and, as she often says, calmness.

To get into a fast mind-set, she has been using Mozart's Sonata for Two Pianos in D Major, which she learned is great, scientifically, for getting people to focus. The evening before her meeting with her boss, she decided to take it easy, turning down a friend's invitation to hang out and going out to dinner by herself and then strolling around the park for a while before driving home. It was still early, maybe around eight or so. She was stopped at a traffic light, waiting for the light to turn green, when another car hit her from behind. No one was hurt, and the accident was little more than a fender bender. It did, however, involve a police report and a trip to the hospital emergency room. She was shook up but thankful that she and the other driver were OK and that her car, though damaged a little, was OK to drive around.

When she was driving back home, still stressed out, the first thing she did was put on her relaxing song, the one from her childhood, her grandmother's song. Who knows how long she listened to it. She just put it on repeat.

She got to work early the next day, so she sat in the parking lot for a while—nervous. She was scheduled to meet with her boss first thing that day. She had her earphones on right until the last minute, switching back and forth between Mozart's sonata and her grandma's song. If she could, she thought, she would wear her earphones right up until seconds before her meeting; that's what she would do. Her head became that music, that rhythm, and she felt at her optimum. She took off the earphones, but she kept playing the music in her head, nonstop all the way to her boss's office. And then there was silence, as if she lost her senses at once. They talked and she explained her thoughts. When the discussion was over, she was mulling over all they had said. Then she heard him announce that a raise seemed appropriate.

What these situations have in common is that both individuals wanted to capture their best mind-set for a specific task at hand. What was key to both was knowing which way their brain waves needed to go to balance into optimum mode. It was a higher frequency all the way for the student, but it was more of a back-and-forth between lower and higher for the library assistant. They both had to have tracks on their playlist to get them there.

Pay Attention to How You Are Feeling

The first thing to do, then, when using your playlist to help you achieve mental balance is to figure out which way you want to send your brain waves. This will depend on how you are feeling at the moment. So, start by taking a mental inventory. Pay attention to how you are feeling. You can usually tell when your mental scale is tipping in one direction (too low or too high) because you feel out of sorts. Maybe it's tipping way too high, and you feel stressed and your temper is short. Or maybe you're jumpy and having a hard time calming down. Maybe it is tipping too low and you feel sapped and sad, which is making it hard to get up to speed. Once you've done some inventory, you can start to identify pieces of music that are capable of moving your balance in one direction or the other (more relaxed and calm or more activated and energized). The goal is to use your music to reset your brain to its optimum performance.

▶▶ In 2008 I was attending a neuroscience conference in San Francisco, and I had a little time to kill. I had a 6:30 p.m. flight out of SFO that night. Although I hadn't gotten a lot of sleep the night before, and I was running on East Coast time, I decided to take a drive up to Napa Valley to a favorite winery in St. Helena, CA, to send back a few special bottles for my wife. The round-trip was about 140 miles long and would take me about four-and-a-half hours' driving time—if traffic cooperated. It was 12:30 and I figured I had enough time to get there, have lunch at the winery, and make a hasty trip back to the airport just in time to get through the gate and catch my flight.

As I started out on my wine trek, I was a bit tired but I was also happy to be back in the Bay Area and driving through some of the most bucolic coastal areas in the country. I was feeling quite good with the level of calm needed to accomplish my goal, but I also needed to be sure that I maintained a high degree of focus on my driving, particularly if I was going to have a glass or two of wine with my lunch. Fortunately, I had my iPod and the personal playlist of songs I use to get my brain activated or relaxed. In this case, I was looking to activate my senses, maintain my good mood, and stay as alert as I possibly could. For the drive up to Napa Valley I listened to some local San Francisco music like Boz Scaggs, Starship, and even some Grateful Dead to relive some of my music from earlier days living and working in Fog City.

To make a long story short, the lunch was good and the wine was excellent, but it was 3:30 and I had at least a two-hour drive to get to the airport. I knew I had to stay focused on and keep my energy and alertness levels up if I was going to make it on time. This is where I pulled out my "On-the-Road-1" playlist

from my iPod. I wasn't looking necessarily for feel-good music for this leg of my trek; I wanted something loud and pounding to activate my thinking brain and pump up my emotions so I could stay on top of my driving, especially in the building traffic as I approached San Francisco. I was also getting quite tired. My "On-the-Road-1" playlist has a combination of music by bands like INXS, the Who, the Foo Fighters, Linkin Park, Sick Puppy, Fourth Quarter Comeback, Attack Attack! and a few others that provide good opportunities to find the right rhythm, beat, and combination of lyrics that have the right meaning for me. With these more upbeat selections, I was able to maintain a balanced mind-set and listen my way through traffic all the way to the airport, where I successfully made my flight on time and was able to sleep most of the way back to D.C.

—Don

Squeezing More Balance Out of Your Tunes

Maximizing each song's ability to affect your brain is something that will be useful to you, and there are many tricks you can use to accomplish this. For now, however, let's zero in on how to increase the amount of balancing power you can achieve from your favorite tunes simply by listening more closely.

The point is that just hearing music is often not enough to trigger its full effects. This is because it's not only hearing music that moves your mind into balance but also actively listening to it that generates the necessary amount of psychic energy to get you there.

(You can use the same listening techniques we'll talk about here to help increase any of the other effects we present in this book as well, so mastering these techniques will help you on various levels in your training.)

Start with Anticipation and Paying Closer Attention

Most of us naturally pay closer attention to how music is being made when we are at live concerts. Live shows have a lot of power over you, so your mind gets into its flow state more easily. To a large extent, this is because you are predisposed to pay closer attention. You go to a concert anticipating that you will be enjoying a quality of sound you can't experience any other way, not in film footage or on sound recordings. Your motivation is spiked. You try to get good seats. You don't want to miss anything. You expect that certain songs will be performed differently during a live performance, and they are unlikely to be repeated in the same way anywhere else. To facilitate these expectations, your brain uses its frontal lobes to make its comparisons between what you anticipate and what is actually happening as you listen. Some of us even use binoculars to enhance what we are able to see, so we can look more closely for the nuances we expect. Every time we spot one, we feel rewarded—so we look and listen even more closely. After a while you are so absorbed in what you are doing that you forget that you are on the hunt for detail, and it's easy to lose track of time as you luxuriate in pleasure. You are flowing with the music and with your quest to take more of it in.

Think about this, about how you listen to live performances. You can and should, however, use these natural motivations, anticipations, and closer listening skills to ramp up the balancing effects of your playlist. Let's take a look at a few ways you can start.

Try Making Comparisons

It's fun to compare songs. Try making a playlist just to exercise your skill in this. Let's pick one of your absolute favorite oldies, one that has probably been covered by other performers. For example, take a song like "All My Loving" by the Beatles. Download the Beatles version as well as a great cover version. Now compare the vocals. Paul McCartney has a very distinctive voice. You might think that the cover version (depending on which one you have) sounds just like him. But on closer listening, you may hear Paul's voice as a little deeper or less boyish. You might notice that his well-known oooh-ooohs at the end are slightly different too. You might think that the Beatles' version is slower. On the other hand, you may think that the cover band gets the guitar playing exact and appreciate or even admire this in them.

The next time you listen to either version, you can practice anticipating these interesting characteristics, and you can catch them as they come up in the tunes. This will put your brain in a mode that will not only increase your pleasure but also speed up the song's balancing effect on you.

If you don't like to listen to cover songs, try downloading and comparing various live versions of a song or a solo version to a version with the full band—say, McCartney's solo performance of "All My Loving" to the Beatles' version. Identify as many differences as you can. Maybe there is an acoustic version of your song that doesn't use any of the background vocals as does the plugged-in version or that features different instruments, as is the case with Bruce Springsteen's "My Hometown." The key to increasing each piece's ability to help balance you, as well as to affect you overall, is to give more attention to how closely you are listening.

The bottom line is that active listening *pays.* The more closely you listen, the more you can involve different areas of your brain. The more additional brain areas you involve, the more strength a song will have to balance you and keep you flowing longer. Remember, once you identify differences in songs, you can then involve your anticipation to further ramp up effects in the future.

Listen with Your Body

Another way you can use a song to induce more balance is to listen with your body. It might sound unusual, but we all did this naturally as children. Imagine a child watching a parade. It's a warm summer day, with tens of thousands of people lining the streets, talking, yelling, and screaming for miles—a unified, rhythmic roar rises above the crowds, and each emerging drum sequence advances until you can feel somersaults in your gut. Fast-forward ten years, that same child is now at his first rock concert—the Dave Matthews Band. Only this time, it is the drums, bass, bright acoustic guitar, and tidal wave of funky electric violin, sax, and piano keys that he's feeling with his body. Remember, music is built into every cell of your body from the beginning, so experiencing it this way is also natural and easy. Genre doesn't matter. Rock, classical, jazz—they all work.

You can orient your attention to the physical details of your body easily just by focusing on how you are breathing. Try taking three deep breaths as you listen to some music. Focus on breathing in through your nose and out of your mouth. Feel the air filling your lungs from the bottom up. A mistake that people often make is to breathe from the top of their lungs. Practice pulling the air in using the bottom of your lungs.

Slow down and relax your breathing as you listen to your music. Imagine the music entering your body as your breath does. Breathe it right in with your own breath. Pay attention to how the music is affecting you. You might think, "This music feels good." Then get more specific. For example, you may like Rusko's "Woo Boost." You may notice that you feel the tune mostly in your upper body and that it spikes your respiration and your energy. You may also notice when this music feels good, like "This song makes me feel more balanced when I am typing but not when I am driving or jogging or have to go meet with someone." You may find that the song works best when you are in an environment where you are alone.

Get to know how music feels in your body and how and when it affects you this way. Knowing this will help you later on when you are trying to match various songs with certain tasks and want to encourage your brain to increase or decrease the frequency of your brain waves to help achieve your goals. You'll have a better idea of how to make playlists that match songs and goals, and you'll be able to use your listening and anticipation skills to enhance their effects.

Playlist Bonus

Try this activity next time you are about to engage in a situation for which you expect an atmosphere of stress or conflict. Listen to a relaxing song or a series of relaxing songs from your playlist for about twenty minutes beforehand. Immediately afterward, follow up with a tune from your playlist that really pumps you up. This will put you right where you need to be to meet the challenge—balanced and flowing.

Feel the Song Emotionally

Another thing you can do to bump up music's ability to balance you is to involve your emotions. For example, Beethoven's "Ode to Joy" may make you feel blissful or Little Richard's "Long Tall Sally" aggressive. Weird Al Yankovic's "Like a Surgeon" may cheer you up (and activate you) or Mark Dinning's "Teen Angel" may make you sad (or slow you down), but "Come On Eileen" by Dexys Midnight Runners might make you happy (or make you feel more active). Try to get a little more precise as to what it is exactly that is moving your energy up or down. That way you can learn to anticipate it or work with it in other ways, such as by looking for the same ingredient in other songs to add to your playlist.

For example, maybe the instrumental part of the song fires your emotions. Maybe you can identify that, for you, it is primarily the violin in "Come On Eileen" that inspires you. Knowing that, you can now anticipate the fiddle's good emotional influence. You can look for nuances. For example, maybe sometimes you hear the violinist playing long and smooth notes, but at other times you hear short, choppy faster ones. And when the notes are very quick and choppy, that specifically is what makes you feel like tapping your foot or dancing—it's what makes you feel good inside. Maybe in another song like "Long Tall Sally" it is the saxophone solo that spikes good vibes or the "woo-hoo" lines that catch you. Or in a song like "Satisfaction" by the Rolling Stones, it is Keith Richards's fuzzy guitar lick that comes in on top of Mick Jagger's lines during the verse, or when all the music drops out and you hear Charlie Watts's drums: wack-wack,

wack-wack-wack, wack-wack, wack-wack-wack. Or maybe it's just the words "no satisfaction" that send your emotions flying.

See the Song

Another way to kick a song's influence on your brain up a few notches is to play a song and summon all kinds of images as the music plays, like watching a movie in your head as you listen to the song. Bring on those images and let them flow: thoughts, pictures, whole scenarios. Some images might be literal, like the bells you hear at the beginning of a song like Bruce Springsteen's version of "Santa Claus Is Coming to Town." Or with Elton John's "Rocket Man," you might image soaring rockets. Some of the images you conjure up may be more abstract, especially with a song like Led Zeppelin's "Stairway to Heaven." Ask yourself, "What would that look like? A stairway? A fog tunnel? A sequence of specific events I see happening in someone's life?"

Sounds—single words, lines and phrases, and even the rhyming or alliteration of words—and their repetition can prompt images for you. Ask yourself which words or sounds inspire which images. This will get you listening more closely overall, thus using more parts of your brain and amplifying a song's effects on your brain.

Look for Meaning

Try identifying the song's theme. Themes can be conveyed via lyrics or music alone. Instrumental themes like Henry

Mancini's "Pink Panther," and Vangelis's *"Chariots of Fire,"* and Tchaikovsky's *The Nutcracker* are good examples. Themes that bubble up from words range from straightforward, like the Rolling Stones' "Satisfaction," to subtler messages, like in Paul Simon's "The Boxer" or Don McLean's "American Pie."

Listening Critically

Listening critically involves being able to identify structure, order, emphases, and so on, as well as to make judgments about how those characteristics of a chosen song make you feel.

There are lots of different ways to do this. For example, you might think about one of your favorite songs and its effects. Take Bassnectar's "Bass Head." Maybe it's the spacious sounds in between the many variations in tempo (speed) that make it easy for you to do something that has a tight rhythm of its own, like typing—or the constant sprinkling of high-pitched sounds and the computerized sound of a tea kettle going off, with hardly any lyrics to the song. Maybe you realize that this all peps you up in a way that keeps your focus wide open to what you are doing.

You can listen critically to your favorite band, group, or orchestra and tune in to one instrument, say, the piano, and explain (in your own interpretation, the only one that matters here) how that single instrument contributes to the whole piece. Then reassemble the piece in your head, melding the piano back into the composition and listening to the unified sound with your ideas about the piano in mind.

You can learn about how a certain piece of music was recorded and think about that the next time you hear it. Or learn about the meaning of the lyrics by reading what the songwriter has to say about them and asking yourself if that explanation has any relevance to your life. You could learn to identify the sound of a specific guitar like the Fender Stratocaster and then listen for its nuances in the songs of some of its iconic players, like Jimi Hendrix, Eric Clapton, and Stephen Stills. You could listen for differences in the legendary sounds of the Gibson SG, played by Carlos Santana in "Evil Ways," The Who's Pete Townsend in "Pinball Wizard," and Angus Young of AC/DC in "You Shook Me All Night Long."

You can learn to pick out instruments: a twelve-string guitar as opposed to a six-string; a stand-up bass, as made popular by the Stray Cats in *Stray Cat Strut*, as opposed to an electric bass; or synthesized trumpets and flutes as opposed to real ones. And then you can offer evaluations of the sounds and their overall combination into the music. For example, "I liked this version because it mentally took me back to..." or, "I think the way Bonnie Raitt played bottleneck guitar in 'Something to Talk About' gave me a strong feeling of determination," or, "The melody in Van Morrison's 'Brown Eyed Girl' and the parallel lyrics makes me feel like..."

Note: We are not suggesting that you have to involve yourself to this extent every time you listen to music, only once in a while to better enhance and tune your brain's responses to the music you love. Remember, closer listening, like all other training methods discussed in this book also becomes more automatic as you practice. So any work you put in now will start kicking in naturally and effortlessly later and can be built upon for long-term use.

Get the Most out of Paying Attention

You don't have to use all these techniques, or even any of them. If you do, however, start using those that come easiest, eventually they will become more automatic, changing the way you listen and react to music. In very little time, you will be able start using your playlist to drive your mental balance whenever and wherever you need, with much greater accuracy, speed, and power.

Putting Together Your Playlist

Here is how to begin choosing songs for a playlist that will help you sustain flow:

▸ **First, pick songs you like a lot.**
▸ **Pay attention to when a certain song works and when it doesn't.**
▸ **Ingrain songs into your memory.**
▸ **Make a playlist that is task oriented. Train your brain with your assembled playlist.**
▸ **Look for new and old songs.** Always important is that the more you like a song, the better it will work. Always be on the lookout for new and old songs that really hit the spot for you. You might take some time during your day to play around on YouTube, checking out old songs you loved in the past. This is

a lot of fun. See if some of those same tunes still have a strong effect on you. You might find covers of those songs by other performers and enjoy them as well. Maybe you will find new songs or other versions by the original performers. Or maybe your search will lead you to new musicians and new tunes via YouTube's recommendations. Don't hesitate to ask friends and family what they are listening to lately. This is a great way to socialize and to gather new material for your playlist.

Exercise

1. **Listen Carefully and Anticipate.** Create a playlist in which you include several short tunes that you've known for a long time will make you feel balanced (meaning at that perfect midpoint between calm and alert) and that you have spent some time actively listening to as described in this chapter. It doesn't matter what the song is, whether it's instrumental or lyrical, just that it's an old favorite and that you enjoy listening to it. Begin playing it once in the morning and again in the afternoon or evening, especially during times you often feel either too mellow or too cranked up. ACTIVELY LISTEN to your song, using as many of the skills discussed in this chapter as you can to break it down and create a mental image from the music. As you listen to the song a few times, pick out a segment that you already really enjoy and focus on your immediate feelings, both in your mind and in your body. Play the song again and anticipate the feel-good segment with an

expectation that you will feel that enjoyment again, and that each time you hear the song, you'll get a little more and longer-lasting pleasure.

Practicing this will train your brain to experience positive feelings when you want them, which in turn will activate your mental processes to reach an optimum state of balance in targeted situations.

The best results should begin to kick in after about two weeks of trying this exercise. After that, use your playlist as needed to help increase or decrease the frequency of your brain waves to keep you in balance as needed.

Playlist Bonus

Research shows that people who combine music with a healthy diet and exercises like yoga, martial arts, walking, or any other physical activity on a consistent basis can achieve even greater results in balancing their wellness.

2. **Use the Power of Musical Cues.** Try using music as a cue for achieving balance before you begin an activity and when you finish an activity. Create a playlist of favorite sounds and songs you can use to help drive your balance for specific activities. You can play the recordings for yourself or, after enough practice, even re-create them in your mind.

How to re-create them? You can create a sound "link" and use it to trigger rebalancing when needed. For example, you can use your pen to tap a certain rhythm (for just a few seconds) on your coffee cup or desk to spark your memory of a certain song. You can hum the song or a certain part of it as well. The idea is to create a sound for yourself that you can mentally link to the song. The more often you do this, the more quickly your brain will respond to the link as it does to the song. Listen to the actual songs in advance and, when appropriate, after activities for positive reinforcement.

Chapter 3

HOW TO USE MUSIC TO ALLEVIATE ANXIETY

The mind is a symphony of neurons playing in unison.

—Don DuRousseau

Calm Your Mind

We have all seen this kind of scene in thrillers: An unsuspecting person (usually female) is home alone. She is awakened in the middle of the night by a sound, usually some slight, distant creaking noise or something dropping to the floor. She gets up to investigate. Everything goes dead silent as she tiptoes down the staircase. One of the stairs squeaks and that mortifies her because she is thinking that someone may detect her approach. As this all-too-recognizable scene goes, she eventually makes her way to a cellar stairwell and heads down, when there is a sudden and loud crash.

She is startled but then sees that it is just a cat jumping off a large box or a water heater. She watches as the cat runs out an open cellar window. "I should have fixed that window," she mutters. She heads back up the stairs, and before she is halfway up, there is another sound, and that's the one that really makes her (and your) skin crawl. Someone attempts to grab her; she slips away and begins running, and this is where the music comes in: a high-pitched, screeching synthesizer starts spitting out unharmonious notes, and deep bass sounds pound a hard, fast, metallic sounding heartbeat—thump thump, thump thump—and then a fast escalating piano sequence begins: 1, 2, 3, 4, 1, 2, 3, 4, 1, 2, 3, 4. Suddenly a synthesizer starts blaring high-pitched chord sequences contrasted with low, pounding bass hits and full piano chords, which come at you in a wall of sound, like the music is being squeezed through a meat grinder—harsh, jagged, and chaotic—and the chase scene begins.

The makers of thriller movies understand the effects of music on visual action, and they are experts in using music to heighten the intensity. As situations like this unfold onscreen, the music helps stimulate our emotions. If you were to mute the volume, much of the emotional connection and anticipation about what's going to happen next would be lost.

Let's look a little closer at what happens in your body when you watch a thriller and hear that scary music. What you are essentially feeling when you watch one of these scenes is music's strong influence over physiological functions, which are driven by the action-regulating parts of the brain. These brain areas are responsible for your fight-or-flight response, and they kick in at any perceived sign of danger. They control functions like increased respiration, heart rate, blood pressure, and the rapid release of adrenaline into the bloodstream. This stimulates the release of NOREPINEPHRINE, a hormone associated with stress, and anxiety-boosting cortisol, a steroid "strength" hormone that mental and physical stress also trigger.

Music can take us the other way too. For example, the opposite effect occurs when you are watching a movie and the score works in combination with certain scenes to induce heightened relaxation and pleasure. Now you feel a spike of the neurochemical DOPAMINE, which is the body's natural feel-good hormone. Dopamine, associated with feelings of self-reward and euphoria, is able to reduce levels of stress by increasing the feeling of pleasure in response to certain thoughts or actions.

Music's Euphoria and Your Calmness

In terms of calming power, dopamine is no placebo—in fact, any of the chemicals washing over your brain is powerful enough to require a license to prescribe. If you were to scan your brain during a cascaded release of dopamine brought on by your listening to a favorite tune, the likeness to a scan of a person using cocaine would be uncanny. Singing, chanting, and even humming can also cause the release of this self-produced brain drug. You just have to like the tune and take pleasure in listening to it or vocalizing it, and your dopamine faucet turns on.

So again, you can use your playlist to take your mind-set up or down. In this chapter, however, our focus is on using music to intensify your ability to induce the appropriate amount of calmness into your daily routines—remembering that your ultimate goal is to always reach balance, that is, your best mind-set for whatever you are doing at the moment. Without balance, your overall performance deteriorates.

We can use music's connection to dopamine to help us reach quicker and deeper states of relaxation. Music helps reprogram our brains because the right songs can pair plea-sure (dopamine release) with our successfully becoming calm. Then we are doubly rewarded (with more dopamine) as we successfully accomplish a goal because we are calm. Your brain gets the message, in effect, that if it calms down in this targeted situation next time around, it will be rewarded. So when the situation next presents itself, your brain anticipates the reward and automatically sends your mind and body instructions to calm down. When it receives its reward, you feel good. And calmness, in that specific situation, has been reinforced. So the next time, and every time thereafter, you will become relaxed even more quickly.

But music's influences are not just chemical. They are elec-trical as well. As we have discussed, the frequency of your brain waves can increase or decrease depending on what you listen to. Music can change your rhythms from those associated with high stress (high beta) to those associated with low stress (alpha and theta) in a few seconds. There are a lot of songs that for one reason or another have this effect on millions of people. One such tune that has brought instantaneous and luxurious relaxation to many is the piano instrumental version of Utada Hikaru's "First Love." This would make a great addi-tion to your playlist (provided you enjoy the tune). There are mounds of research, as well, showing that listening to Mozart also reduces anxiety, balances the mind, and improves overall performance skills for most people. The trick, as always, is to find the music that works best for you. If these work for you, we recommend you add them to your playlist for calmness. You'll feel the calming effects you induce with your playlist throughout your entire body.

Irritable bowel syndrome, Crohn's disease, and celiac disease are illnesses linked to chronic stress and anxiety. Each of these conditions has detrimental long-term consequences, including allergic and inflammatory problems that can lead to heart and cardiovascular conditions and increased risk of diabetes and stroke. And that's just the tip of the iceberg—the list of conditions brought about by negative reactions to high stress goes on and on. Muscle tension, poor circulation through shallow breathing, and decreased heart rate are further problems that can complicate existing medical conditions and lead to other illnesses, like fibromyalgia, which lead to reduced activity levels and may exacerbate symptoms of depression. These links have been made over and over. So as you make your mind stronger and more peaceful, your physical health will improve as well.

Playlist Bonus

Select music that you already sense will induce a state of calm. Use imagery to ramp up its calming effects. Consciously associate the pleasure gained from your music (dopamine release) with a reduction in your anxiety. This trains your brain to seek the pleasure itself and to seek the feeling of less stress. Train as close as possible (in time and place) to your targeted goal—for example, if you get anxious when you are stuck in traffic, play your relaxing tune(s) then, right there. Your brain and body will begin to experience subtle changes in character and makeup. With enough practice, this training can drive the brain's plasticity and make changes in your ability to calm yourself in general and in a targeted situation for the long-term. You will start feeling a positive change after doing this in as little as two weeks.

There are many types of stress and anxiety: ones we expect and deal with daily, like obligations, deadlines, and new projects, and unexpected ones, like computer crashes, delayed information processing, and interpersonal flair-ups. Our job is to improve our reaction to both.

Under normal circumstances, your brain produces a mix of frequencies that are quite balanced in location and occurrence across the two cerebral hemispheres, thus creating a BRAIN ACTIVITY PATTERN (BAP) that's quite stable over time. We can change from a pattern consistent with rumination (overthinking) to a pattern consistent with a more relaxed mindset or even meditation. What's overthinking? Let's say you had a turbulent conversation with your boss, and you can't stop thinking about it for several reasons, including fear that you may have damaged your good relationship with her. In this case, you can use music to drive the brain's thinking, emotional, and reward systems.

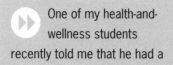

One of my health-and-wellness students recently told me that he had a run-in with one of his professors. He feared that he had ruined his relationship with that professor for the rest of the semester. On the way home he stopped and got himself a latte, thinking that maybe he could think the situation through. It didn't work. Instead, he couldn't stop thinking about what had passed. When he got home, he realized that if he was to find a solution to his problem, he would have to calm himself down first—and especially get his mind off of what had happened and move on to what could be done about it.

I had recently given a lecture on turning your iPod into a brain-training machine, and so he figured, "Why not try it?" He didn't have a playlist at the time, so instead he located some CDs in his music collection that he thought might calm him down. He put on Dire Straits' "Romeo and Juliet," and it started to calm him down. So he played it again, just closing his eyes and breathing slower to the beat of the music. He latched on to certain lyrics like "dream" and "the time was wrong" and "how

about it." And that last line, "how about it," swept him and his fear away. So he put on an old favorite, "Across the Universe" by the Beatles. The musician he related to the most was John Lennon, and he sang the song with a mellow positivity. He responded especially to the line "Nothing's gonna change my world" and sang along each time it came around.

The lyrics seemed to reassure him that there was nothing to fear. Much more relaxed, he put on "Imagine," and that did the trick, so he kept playing it until he felt better and confident that everything would be all right. He had succeeded in calming himself and, in doing so, had dissolved the negative compulsive thoughts that had imbalanced him before. Flowing again, he was able to compose, in his mind, the conversation he would have with his professor that would right things for them both.

—Joseph

To bring your highly stressed brain back to a balanced state of flow, you need to focus your attention on calming down. This is why students, businesspeople, athletes, and professionals of all types love listening to music to calm their mind (and body) before important proceedings or at the end of a busy day.

Power Up with Imagery

If you think about your past, you might remember times when you were vigorously on top of your game and your mind was perfectly relaxed. You can use those memories and images to help you reach a great sense of calm anytime. By combining specific songs from your playlist with your own positive memories and images, it's possible to make valuable changes in your brain's neurochemistry and train your brain so that you can call on those memories and images for extra oomph as needed.

Imagery works best when you pair it with songs you feel some emotion about. The more emotional significance a song has for you, the more it can influence the changes in your brain that will help you reach perfect calm. This works because there are strong connections in your brain between the visual image your mind creates while you listen to a song and the way the music actually drives the scene you are creating in your head.

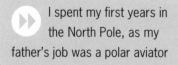

I spent my first years in the North Pole, as my father's job was a polar aviator pilot. It was the sound—or even more exact, the music—of silent, white, bright snow that formulated for me a connection with eternity—that kind of feeling you get when you feel like a particle of the universe.

Even though I remember all the lullabies my mom was singing for me before sleep time, the most powerful musical memory that is deeply ingrained in my brain is that of white, bright snow. In the morning, before the sled pulled by deer or dogs would take me to a local preschool, I would head outside. I'd take our small station fox, little white bear, or my Siberian husky Mars and absorb that magnificent music of white silence. My parents would ask me to come in and wait in a warm hut, but I'd insist on staying out, so they eventually gave up and just dressed me warm. I would always smile, as it was a secret only I knew, something between myself and that raw white nature. I would always tell my mother the same thing (in Russian), "No line, no border—there is no end; this is it."

On my life journey, I've tapped into that memory so many times to arrive at my best mental focus. It doesn't matter if it's learning, teaching, taking tests, doing sports, dancing, playing music, speaking publicly; I can use that white, blank power. I recently asked my daughter, a graduate of New York University who now loves to perform and teach yoga classes professionally, "How is your practice doing? Do you feel you are getting better in what you do?" The answer was, "I think so, but you know, Mom, there is no finish line."

—Galina

As a song generates an image in your mind, your memory can easily evoke additional images to script the direction your mind-movie will take. Pleasurable images emit dopamine. This rewards your experience—of using imagery and music in general and of using the scenario you have just scripted. In addition more specifically, it trains your memory to call up the scene for you next time. The more you repeat your mind-movie, the more easily, quickly, and powerfully you will experience its effects. Ultimately, through repetition, it will become automatic and will trigger for you when you need it to.

Try using a favorite song to make your own calming mind-movie today. If you are unable to immediately think of a perfect scenario to play in your mind as you listen to your selected calming song, don't worry. Start slowly. Begin by listening to a piece of music you know well, and then start anywhere, recalling any kind of scenario in which you felt relaxed and performed at your optimum. Then play the tune again and try to add more detail. Do this three or four times in a row. Add more detail to the scene each time. The experience should give you a song to play and something to build on in the future when you're trying to increase feelings of calm.

Lessening the Power of Stressful Memories

Sometimes unpleasant memories enter your calm mind-set uninvited, and you just can't get rid of them. They not only disrupt your calmness, but they also stress you out, lower your mood, and change your blood chemistry so that it works to produce further stress. They spike blood pressure, heart rate, respiration, and so on. All this tips your balance and derails your flow.

You can, however, use your playlist in combination with guided imagery to reset your brain and help stop your stressful memory from recurring. The way this works is really neat. We know that when you recall a memory, it carries the same emotional weight it had when you last remembered it. But here's what we can do with music. Although a memory comes to your mind with certain emotional intensity, you can treat it right then and there (with your favorite song and positive imagery) and dilute it. Next time the unpleasant memory invades you, it will be less severe than before because you have watered it down. Your job is to repeat the treatment until you have completely diluted that memory's effect.

Say you have stored in memory a picture of a sad event and that memory keeps coming back at you and stressing you out. You can, with a little practice, learn to challenge your memory of that event with a piece of music, one that evokes completely opposite emotions and images, one that brings you self-confidence and gives you pleasure.

For example, someone we know was able to reverse recurring sad memories brought on by her mother's passing by playing Sam Cooke's 1962 hit "Twistin' the Night Away." The song, one of her mother's favorites, evoked huge and beautiful memories of her and her mother twisting in the kitchen when she was just nine years old and everything was good and safe. After a little practice, the song was able to instantly replace pain with pleasure and grief with goodness and joy. It's not easy, though, as your brain has a tendency to do things by going through the same circuit it has used in the past.

Imagine, for example, that you have taken the same route to work for ten years, and today you decide you want to take a different route from now on. Can you take this different route? Sure you can—you just need some time to commit it to memory, or you will divert back to your old habit, your old circuit.

So if you are trying to reverse a stressful emotional memory with music, you have to do plenty of reps. Most people report positive effects in two to three weeks.

Playlist Bonus

If you are trying to reverse a stressful memory and want to ramp up the effect of your calming tune, after you play it several times, follow it up with a piece of energizing music.

Remember, you have to repeat this kind of reversing strategy aggressively for your brain to rewire its connections, dissolve that stressful memory, and create a new connection to offer you happiness and pleasure instead. However, you can do it. With time, your new memory, which you have chosen, can significantly lessen the pain and, in some cases, can completely erase the previous memory, as well as any negative feelings around the event that accompanied it.

Triumph over Conflict

The Russian figure skaters Ekaterina Gordeeva and her husband Sergei Grinkov essentially won every competition they ever entered, including gold medals in both the 1988 and 1994 Olympics. Then tragedy struck in 1995, in Lake Placid,

New York, when Sergei died suddenly (and unexpectedly) while practicing on the ice for a *Stars on Ice* tour. This was only one year after the couple had made skating history, winning Olympic gold for the second time. Sergei was only twenty-eight years old at the time of his death, and Ekaterina was twenty-four. The two had begun skating together as children, had fallen in love, had married in 1991, and had their daughter Darya in 1992, three years before Sergei's untimely heart attack. Ekaterina's loss was mourned throughout the world and would be dramatic for her in many, many ways. Yet in February 1996, after long repeated training using movement, music, and the many postured images of her dance, she was on the ice again. This time she skated as a solo performer, in a televised tribute performance to her husband. Her own assessment of the performance was that she felt "double strong" because she felt that her husband was with her. All of the rehearsals skating to the long, slow notes of Gustav Mahler's Symphony No. 5, and especially her performance, helped Ekaterina keep her mind flowing. Together they created a new source of memory she could summon whenever she needed. All of us who saw the performance could feel its healing power in our hearts.

There are as many stories of human triumph over grief and conflict as there are people in the world. We all have seen one: people hit with the worst of circumstances, walking away triumphant, stronger, more self-aware, and more on course than ever. We have also, unfortunately, seen the reverse: people devastated by conflict and catastrophe.

It is clear that when talking about anxiety, there is a scale of magnitude. The death of a spouse or family member is of greater stress than upsetting your boss. And upsetting your boss is more stressful than not finding a parking spot at the shopping mall. But it's equally clear that responses to similar stressors can completely flip one person's world, whereas another individual might find a coping mechanism within himself or herself to get through the tough times and move forward.

The most important factor that contributes to the way you handle stress, however, is your actual strategy for coping—your ability to let go and get back in the flow.

Two Ways of Dealing with Stress

There are two common ways people attempt to deal with stress. One way is negative; the other is positive.

Consider the following: On one end of town, there is a young man who feels he is stuck in a dead-end job. He recently interviewed for new employment and has just received a call saying that he was not selected for the position. He crawls into his bedroom at home to be by himself, starts smoking again (which he gave up not so long ago), drinks more heavily at night, acts moody at his job—which he doesn't like but is the only employment he has—and ultimately starts fighting with his wife and children and other family members. The conflict and stress in his life are clear, yet in most cases, his situation would register below the median mark of extreme stressors. But his reaction to his situation isn't helping him; in fact, it's only adding to his internal and external conflicts, moving him farther away from his long-term goal of a job he likes and financial stability.

On the other end of town, there is a young, athletic woman whose passion is kung fu. She has been prepping for a tournament she has her heart set on competing in, but she recently was diagnosed with a potentially terminal form of leukemia. She must wait for more tests and procedures and a fuller prognosis. Her stressors are completely off the charts. The competition is on her calendar and has been for nearly a year. Her doctor has given her a green light to participate in the event. So she rehearses every day and luxuriates in her practice, which is to perfect an old and beautiful kung-fu form. The form (a sort of dance) includes many extremely long, spiraling, and graceful lines—which call to her mind images of freedom and strength and peace. The music she selects sends her mind reeling with images of an eagle floating over mountaintops, peacefully, elegantly, and powerfully. The sounds are gentle and smooth, with modern and rich synthesized strings and long, flowing notes to match her movements—which amps up her feeling of balance and ingrains it more deeply. When she rehearses, she feels so much psychic energy that she flows from one posture to another with great strength. She becomes the eagle. Watching her, you would never think there could be anything troubling her. And in her mind, while she performs and for long periods after, she feels purified of trouble. She performs every movement as though it were the only movement in the universe and enters into even greater energetic levels of creativity and joy. Her illness has no chance of stealing her calm or flow. In fact, with her, as with Ekaterina, it is all quite the opposite: she has become stronger.

▶▶ There is the song "Feeling of Falling" by Bonnie Raitt. I like to use this song when I'm feeling a little bit down or anxious about the unknowns in my life. There's something about the music and lyrics by artists like Bonnie, and many others like her, that help me find the feeling I'm looking for in the words of the song. This helps me bond with the music and envision what my goals are, which might be to relax or to just realize that someone else can be going through what I am, and knowing this helps me calm down and refocus my balance. For me, I've learned to anticipate the repeating lyric "I miss that feeling of falling, falling on over the ledge" and I use it to realize that sometimes falling into the unknown is not a bad thing, as possibly the unknown can bring great reward and satisfaction. Realizing this helps me relax and continue to deal with the changes in my life.

—Don

By repeating her rehearsals again and again, she has paired music, imagery, movement, and reward with her goal of a perfect performance. She has trained her body and mind to stay flowing.

Being able to get yourself into this mind-set enables you to transform anxiety into calm. For some people, it can mean the ability to transform the potential of hell on earth into paradise.

This is important and empowering. Research shows that the challenging details in such experiences, when met with your belief that you have the skill to meet the task successfully, actually heighten the flow mind-set even further and sustain it longer. Individuals who demonstrate such triumphs are survivors. They are heroes. And we admire them because we can relate to their desire to overcome anxiety and misery. Their victory gives us hope and pride. It puts before us the power of flow.

It is true that various things in life can launch us into flow—but music is perhaps the simplest to work with because it has been built into every cell of our being.

Sample Playlists for Inducing Calm

Let's take a look at one individual's playlists, which she uses several times a day at work. She uses individual songs, often repeated several times, that match specific stressful situations that may arise. Seeing how she has arranged songs to suit her personal needs may help you in making your own playlists. We encourage you to create your own and experiment a lot.

Sample "General Calm" Playlist

▸ **"The Splendour,"** Pantha du Prince (unclutters my head)

▸ **Pachelbel's Canon in D Major** (was played at my wedding and spurs great memories)

▸ **"Diamond in the Rough,"** Shawn Colvin (gives me images of things I can hold on to)

▸ **"Every Breath You Take,"** Police (very visceral rhythm that makes my whole body and mind relax)

▶ **"Here Comes the Sun,"** Beatles (enhances my positivity as it calms me and brings me images of many happy mornings when I was a kid without a care in the world)

Sample "Heavy Calm" Playlist

▶ **Delta Waves Music,** Modern Meditation Series Download

▶ **Deep Meditation**—Beta, Alpha, Theta, & Delta Waves, Kelly Howell

▶ **Brain Music Therapy "Relaxing"** track (we'll go into BMT more in Chapter 10)

The songs included in the preceding playlists are, of course, customized for use by the individual who created them and for her particular life situations. We use it here only to illustrate how someone familiar with our techniques has formulated a playlist that works—for her. Your playlist will depend on your own life situations, current needs, stressors, your personal response to stressors, and especially the music you personally love. However, the guiding idea, behind using your playlist (and this sample) is to relax your mind when you need to. Furthermore, when you use it regularly in targeted situations that cause you stress, your playlist will change your response to those situations. It will reprogram your brain to react differently to your personal life stressors, shutting them down one at a time—with each proactive step you take. As a few days of training turn into a few weeks, you will begin to see more positive results and will feel less stressed about what has been causing you pain. And as weeks turn into months and then into a year, you will feel much greater stress reduction and experience a whole new you.

When your mind is flowing, you won't be stressed out. Let your playlist take you there.

Putting Together Your Playlist

Here is how to begin choosing songs for a playlist that will help you alleviate anxiety.

- **First, pick songs you like a lot.**
- **Pay attention to when a certain song works and when it doesn't.**
- **Ingrain songs into your memory.**
- **Make a playlist that is task oriented. Train your brain with your assembled playlist.**
- **Look for new and old songs.**
- **Listen closely and anticipate.**
- **Look for calming songs.** Start by choosing any kind of music (according to your taste) that generally calms your anxiety. If you experiment a little, you can develop some real precision in picking the right songs to relax you in specific situations. Sometimes, your mind and body instantly recognize what music you need at just that moment to soothe you. Select from those songs first. But then also try listening to a variety of other songs you believe can more exactly relate to your specific needs at

the moment. For example, are you on your way to meet with your boss, or are you headed to take a test? Are you angry or sad or anxious? Are there songs that instill calm into you, given where you are and your goal? Begin tracking how specific songs change certain moods and how they leave you feeling in specific situations. Add these to your anxiety-busting playlist. You can even make situation-specific playlists for breaking down anxiety, such as "Before Public Speaking" or "Before Office Meetings."

Exercise

1. **Track Your Blood Pressure and Heart Rate.** Try using a blood-pressure machine, available at a variety of stores, to track both blood pressure and heart rate. If you pay close attention, you will notice that some songs on your playlist will increase blood pressure and heart rate, and others will decrease them. Be sure to slow down your breathing, using the suggestions given earlier in this chapter, as you use your blood-pressure machine. Chart your calming songs and indicate which have the greatest effect on you, at what time of day, and where. In this way, you can better match your songs with your desired results. Note that the combination of slowing your breathing and listening to a relaxing tune will coordinate your mind and body to calm down more quickly and deeply. Results are typically greatest if you experienced a lot of stress or were irritable and cranky before listening.

2. **Use a Five-Star System.** Create a chart using a five-star system, where 1 is the lowest and 5 is the highest, by asking yourself, "How relaxed do I feel after hearing this song?" In general, people find songs that are slower in tempo and pensive more relaxing. Songs in this category can range from Pink Floyd's "I'm Growing Numb" to Brahms's "Lullaby."

3. **Use Expectation, Recollection, and Imagery.** Choose a tune you've known for a while and enjoy. Longer and slower songs will yield better results. As you play the song, bring to mind a favorite positive memory, either already associated with the song or one you want to now connect with the song. With your memory in mind, bring your thoughts to the forefront. Try to make them clearer in your mind and more real. Think about the details of that memory and how you felt, and start to imagine that you are back in that same place. Each time you listen to this piece of music, try to take yourself back to where you were, and begin to let go of any thoughts that stress you out, those that currently occupy your mind. By focusing on slowing your breathing to six or eight deep breaths per minute as you listen and visualize, you can further reduce your level of stress. As you learn to use your memory to imagine yourself reliving a pleasant past experience, your positive emotions will reduce the release of stress producing chemicals in the brain.

Chapter 4

HOW MUSIC CAN INCREASE YOUR ALERTNESS

Music cleanses the understanding,
inspires it, and lifts it
into a realm which it could not
reach if it were left to itself.

—Henry Ward Beecher

We all look for that extra energy boost every now and then. For many of us, the first places to grab it are coffee, energy drinks, pills, and exercise (when we have time). But music can also give you the lift you're looking for, without any of the negative side effects, and you can carry it right in your pocket.

We have been talking in previous chapters about how your brain waves have the ability to synchronize themselves to a piece of music and how higher-frequency brain waves are associated with greater arousal and focus. Now, let's take a look at another property of music: beats per minute (BPM), which can play a role in increasing alertness. When we talk about BPM, we are referring to how many beats per minute occur in a given song. For example, "Born This Way" by Lady Gaga has a moderately high BPM of 124. Generally speaking a BPM of 124 could moderately boost your arousal. For context, the low end of the spectrum is something like Sinatra's "New York, New York," which runs at leisurely 27 BPM. At the other extreme, a song like the Knack's "My Sharona" thumps in at 150 and the Ramones' "I Wanna Be Sedated" at 165.

There are several ways you can figure out a song's BPM. The easiest is to use any search engine and plug in these keywords: "artist," "song title," "BPM." This will lead you to sites that list the BPM of the song you are looking for and sometimes to sites that house BPM charts for whole libraries of songs.

You can also use the old-fashioned way (learning how this works helps you understand the basics of BPM, and it works on your close listening skills). To find BPM this way, you simply count every bass-drum kick you hear for thirty seconds, and then double that number. If you play the tune on YouTube, the prompt will display how many seconds have passed as the song plays, which can make it even easier to keep track.

Here's an unusual way to count BPM that can be enjoyable if you are in a playful mood: Try going to the website Handy Software Tools (http://www.all8.com/tools/) and listen to a recording of your favorite tune (using your iPod or MP3 or anything else, including singing the tune yourself). Then tap out the beats using any key on your keyboard. A digital prompt on your computer screen will give you the BPM—no need for a watch. You'll have a little fun and increase your listening skills as you do it—and the next time you hear your song. The method is fairly accurate, and it doesn't really matter if you are off by a few beats, because BPM listings for songs are often given ranges anyway (e.g., 90–100).

If you really get into it, there are several other BPM program downloads that provide more sophisticated software that is completely automatic and can give you readings without having to tap. One of these is iTunes BPM detection, beaTunes, which gives you a song's BPM and can analyze all the songs in your library (for BPM), as well as help you build as many customized playlists as you want based on BPM. There are many other kinds of software as well. It's easy to find one that works for you.

There is a lot you can do with a BPM measurement. For example, many people like to make playlists to use to reach various levels of alertness, for example, "High Alert," "Higher Alert," "Highest Alert." These playlists come in handy because different tasks throughout the day call for more (or sometimes less) mental energy. The different playlists allow you to more accurately prescribe what you need according to each situation. For instance, getting awake in the morning may require more energy than having a conversation with a coworker during lunch. Writing and sending a report to your bosses can take more energy than anything else you'll do all day. So the level of alertness you need to get yourself in your best flowing mind-set varies per task, time, place, and so on. And you can creatively use BPM to increase the effectiveness of your playlists to help you accomplish this.

The idea is to match your playlists with specific daily tasks so that you can operate at your best.

BPM: A Case Study

Let's take a look at some sample playlists that illustrate how one individual used BPM to arrange songs for high, higher, and highest alert to address his needs. Remember, these are just samples of how someone else who is familiar with our techniques has used the concepts. As always, your selections should reflect your own tastes.

The playlists here feature a variety of music. You can do something similar or use all the same genre. You may find that playing just one specific song over and over, such as Huey Lewis and the News' "The Power of Love," gives you the mind-set you want for a certain level of alert. Go with it. (Whatever you discover about how a song affects you, write it down, because if you are like the rest of us, you will forget.) Put that song on your iPod or MP3 player, and play it every time you need it. This will help your brain remember the song, speed up its recall of the song, and start rewiring itself to give you the

> ▸▸ A student of mine was recently finishing up some research in one of our computer labs. When he came into the room, he had on a set of headphones, and you could hear he was playing music. He had been listening to me talk for months, during the writing of this book, about how music can launch your mind into a highly energized focus, and he said he was giving it a try. "How did it work?" I asked him. "Great," he said. I asked him what he was listening to. He said, "I made a playlist of anything I liked that had BPM over 150."
>
> —Joseph

alertness you want when you want it. What's more, your brain will reward itself with a dopamine cocktail and make it all even easier the next time.

Notice that each of the playlists here is arced (arranged from lowest to highest) according to BPM. The intention is to increase levels of alertness by increasing each successive song's BPM.

Sample "High Alert" Playlist (100–130 BPM)

▸ **"Pride (The Name of Love),"** U2 (106)

▸ **"Lady Madonna,"** Beatles (110)

▸ **"Goodbye Earl,"** Dixie Chicks (120)

▸ **"Sweet Dreams,"** Marilyn Manson (128)

▸ **"Don't Phunk with My Heart,"** Black Eyed Peas (130)

Sample "Higher Alert" Playlist (135–155 BPM)

▸ **"Back on the Chain Gang,"** Pretenders (138)

▸ **"Beat It,"** Michael Jackson (139)

▶ **"We Didn't Start the Fire,"** Billy Joel (145)

▶ **"The Power of Love,"** Huey Lewis and the News (155)

▶ **"Authority Song,"** John Mellencamp (155)

Sample "Highest Alert" Playlist (160–175+ BPM)

▶ **"Rebel Yell,"** Billy Idol (167)

▶ **"Johnny B. Goode,"** Chuck Berry (169)

▶ **"Jailhouse Rock,"** Elvis Presley (171)

▶ **"Long Tall Sally,"** Little Richard (174)

▶ **"Rock This Town,"** Stray Cats (204)

Extra-High BPM Tracks (play loudly!)

▶ **"The Happening,"** The Supremes (197)

▶ **"Boys of Summer,"** The Ataris (201)

▶ **"Watershed,"** Indigo Girls (203)

Let's take a look at a different situation and hence a different kind of playlist. Say you are rested but bored out of your mind or completely unmotivated. Try creating a playlist that combines all three alertness levels into one list and arc them. This will give you a buildup effect. You may want to use songs that you like to dance to.

Sample "Getting Unbored" Playlist (play loudly!)

▶ **"Goodbye Earl,"** Dixie Chicks (120)

▶ **"Back on the Chain Gang,"** The Pretenders (138)

▶ **"Rebel Yell,"** Billy Idol (167)

▶ **"Jailhouse Rock,"** Elvis Presley (171)

▶ **"Boys of Summer,"** The Ataris (201)

If you have the room, get up and dance, and maybe try some air guitar or lip-synching. The combination of sound and movement will ramp up the music's effects on your mind and body. This gives you a way of redirecting your thoughts and actions into a state of flow.

Here's another situation where you can use your BPM playlists. Let's say that you receive an unexpected business email. Imagine it is from a new client with a big problem. You're tired, however, and you need an immediate dose of clear, uplifting energy—there's no time to wait; you need to alert your mind as well as avoid frustration. You can't afford to say something wrong or come off as dismissive. You don't want to use coffee or prescription medication. You don't need to. If you have already conditioned yourself with some targeted alert playlists, it's possible to immediately shift from a lower-focused mind-set to a higher-flowing alertness. Just pick the level of alertness you require from your "High," "Higher," and "Highest" playlists, play your fix is ready-made.

As with any kind of effect we've discussed in this book, what's key is getting your playlists set up in advance. This way you have what you need right there in your pocket. Then train your brain by using your lists, over and over.

Remember also to listen closely to your music selections. This will help you squeeze more juice out of them. It will also help you figure out how different songs, singers, bands, and even types of music work better for one task over another. For example, you might discover that the Ataris' cover of "Boys of Summer" is terrific to alert you in most situations when you require major fuel to jet you into motion, but Don Henley's original version of the same song works best for your typical drive home after work. This sort of difference is more common than you think.

Don't forget about balance or you can slip out of flow.

BPM and Exercise

Playlists based on BPM are also very effective for boosting your alertness and motivation in athletic activities. Again, the combination of music and movement will supercharge you. If you enjoy jogging, biking, swimming, weight lifting, aerobics, or any other sporting activities, you can use your playlists to pump you up to your optimal performance. Up-tempo music, with 100 to 130 BPMs and even faster, is usually best. The best tunes have a hard, driving, easy-to-follow, and easy-to-anticipate beat. This kind of beat activates your brain and synchronizes the movements of your muscles to the pounding rhythms. So you are getting a double effect—a flowing mind and flowing muscles.

Say you like to use a treadmill. A basic treadmill workout, for example, generally responds well to tunes of 150 BPM, but you can go up as high as 170 or more and still coordinate your movement with the tempo.

The following are generally suggested BPM ranges for various activities combining music and exercise:

- Under 100 BPM: Slow workouts, warm-ups, and cooldowns
- 115–120 BPM: Light walking (stroll pace)
- More than 130–140 BPM: Power walking and cardio
- 135–160 BPM: Jogging
- 150–175 BPM: Running
- More than 175 BPM: Fast running and sprinting

Note: Remember to always consult your physicians before beginning any exercise program.

Once you're an advanced user, you might want to arc your selections so that speedier and more powerful tempos kick in when you need them most in your routine, placing a slower, feel-good piece at the end—or sprinkled throughout as needed—to help you cool down and balance your mind and body.

Other Factors to Consider

There are other musical components that can ˴affect alertness besides BPM. These include a song's lyrics, any emotions a song sparks in you, and images that emerge in your mind. Generally speaking, you want to find something you can identify with: the words have the right meaning, the beat is at the right tempo for your mood, any emotions the song brings up work in sync to raise alertness to the level you want, and there are riffs or a chorus that you can focus on and anticipate in the song. The more you can fine-tune your selections, the more potential they have for quickly increasing your alertness.

When you weigh all these factors into the mix, however, you can see why BPM, though important, isn't everything. This is why you might have a song with a BPM of more than 200, like the Stray Cats' "Rock This Town," that doesn't arouse alertness for you, when a song like "One of Us" by Joan Osborne, with a BPM of only 87, sends you flying high. If a low BPM and melody, words, and theme all really excite you and bring to mind images of good days and exhilarated positive feelings, then that song could prove more effective than the faster tune—at least for you, and for certain tasks. So you need to be aware of and consider these other factors when using music to heighten your alertness.

In addition, it would be a mistake to assume that a certain piece of music will always work for you. Sometimes the reason is simple: you might just be too distracted or tired and just can't concentrate. At times like these, it might be better to find some relaxing music and try to get a short nap and then try again a bit later to raise your alertness level and get your mind flowing.

At other times, however, you don't have the luxury of shutting down and taking a nap because the demands of work, family, and life in general don't permit it. In cases like this, having a premade playlist that you have trained your brain to respond to can be the best way to deliver what you need.

Peak flow, remember, can be achieved when the characteristics of your song strike the right balance—that is, the targeted music is exciting and makes you feel not only good but also more alert and aware about the task at hand.

One song I use to increase my alertness is the Beatles' "Shout," which was actually written by the Isley Brothers. "Shout" is well known (it was in the movie *Animal House*), and it has all the elements of a song that easily gets me excited: it's repetitive (highly), I understand and can bond with the lyrics, "shout, kick your heels up and shout, throw your hands back and shout," and it makes me want to sing and dance, which energizes my brain and makes me more alert.

The key is to actually do it, to sing and dance, or at least to mentally go through the motions with the goal of being more attentive and in focus when it's over. Sometimes, I might even play it twice in a row.

—Don

A Jogger's Sample Playlist

Let's take a look at a playlist from an individual who is familiar with our techniques. He uses the following playlist for jogging every other day. Seeing how he has arranged his songs to suit his personal needs may help you make your own playlists.

The idea for this playlist first came to him from hearing a sequence of four songs on his car radio as he was driving in to work one day. The songs and the order they were played had a terrific effect on his alertness and put him into a state of flow instantly. The four songs were old but ones he used to enjoy a lot and hadn't heard in a while. He played them in this order: "Get Together," by the Youngbloods; "Brown Eyed Girl," by Van Morrison; "Margaritaville," by Jimmy Buffet; and "Good Lovin'," by the Rascals. When he got to work, he wrote down the titles so that he could put together a playlist for his iPod. He couldn't wait to try them out jogging.

When he did, he wasn't surprised at how well they worked together. Although, he *was* surprised at how much he enjoyed starting out on the slower side with "Get Together," which contrasted with the faster songs that followed. The contrast amplified the excitement the quicker songs brought on. So that inspired him.

Soon he added other oldies to the playlist. As time rolled on, his original four songs moved around. He tried letting the iPod shuffle songs for a while, but that didn't go so well. When using that, he began anticipating the songs that he didn't want to hear and hoping they wouldn't play. The shuffle feature had turned his jog into a sort of Russian roulette. One good aspect of the shuffle, though, was that it let him taste various ways of organizing the songs into sequences he might not have used. For example, one day a slower tune came up just as he approached the halfway mark of a four-mile jog. He let it play through, and when a faster and then even faster tune followed, he noticed that the sequence gave him just what he needed at that point in the jog.

He also discovered two very important things using his oldies playlist. First, BPM mattered, but there didn't have to be just one arc to the playlist. There could be several, giving him rests and pick-me-ups where he needed them. So he was learning to match his songs with what he was actually feeling on his jog—and when. The second thing he discovered was that sometimes his emotional connection to a tune could-have much more influence on alertness than BPM, especially if it was a song that sent his imagination wild with fantastic-feeling imagery.

For example, Don McLean's "American Pie" had this effect on him. You might not expect that, because it has a low BPM of 96. But for him, he remembered playing a concert with McLean when he was in college. McLean had played first, and he had played with his band second. For all practical purposes, no one really knew who McLean was back then, including him. Toward the end of his awesome set, McLean introduced a song that had not come out yet. It was titled "American Pie." Of course, he blew everyone away, particularly "the jogger" and his band. The jogger was totally enraptured by the song. Neither he nor his band wanted to go on after that. Can you imagine? Sometime later, he was in the dorms and someone had his radio up loud, and he heard the song again. Then he started hearing it every day all day long. "What a hit! What a fantastic piece of work!" he thought. And he fell in love with "American Pie" all over again. He still loves that song today, with all the memories of that concert and McLean running through his head whenever he hears it. So when he jogs, that song can send him into a sprint if he wants it to.

In working out his "Jogging" playlist, he learned that paying attention to BPM pays. But he also learned to pay attention to the emotional connections you have to your tunes. You can use that connection to kick your alertness up several notches. Besides, an emotional connection can give you the opportunity to relive pleasant memories in your head like good movies with great soundtracks.

You'll notice that there is a song that repeats at the end of the jogger's playlist. This allows him to bring emotion, BPM, and the anticipation of that song coming up all together to crescendo his jog.

Sample "Jogging" Playlist

▶ **"Get Together,"** Youngbloods (104)

▶ **"Let's Spend the Night Together,"** The Rolling Stones (140)

▶ **"Brown Eyed Girl,"** Van Morrison (109)

▶ **"All My Loving,"** #1 Beatles Cover Band (117)

▶ **"Margaritaville,"** Jimmy Buffet (124)

▸ **"Born to Be Wild,"** Steppenwolf (147)

▸ **"So You Want to Be a Rock 'n' Roll Star,"** The Byrds (154)

▸ **"Blowin' in the Wind,"** Bob Dylan (150)

▸ **"Tambourine Man,"** The Byrds (122)

▸ **"Chimes of Freedom,"** The Byrds (128)

▸ **"Song Sung Blue,"** Neil Diamond (110)

▸ **"Good Lovin',"** Young Rascals (195)

▸ **"Turn, Turn, Turn,"** The Byrds (124)

▸ **"American Pie,"** Don McLean (96)

▸ [Repeat] **"Let's Spend the Night Together,"** The Rolling Stones (140)

The jogger's cooldown is usually made up of stretches, slow walking, and/or tai chi, with five to ten minutes of slow, very mellow, meditative delta-wave synthesizer sounds on a separate playlist on his iPod. And he walks away feeling like a million bucks.

Although his BPM list doesn't match the BPM prescription provided earlier in this chapter, it allows him to ease into his jog and then pumps him up and slows him down as he needs it—for now. At the moment, his playlist is a work in progress, suited to his mind and body.

We encourage you to be flexible in setting up your playlists. In the end, numbers are just numbers, suggestions and general markers to inspire you. So whatever works for you, go with it.

Putting Together Your Playlist

Here is how to begin choosing songs for a playlist that will help increase your alertness.

▸ **First, pick songs you like a lot.**
▸ **Pay attention to when a certain song works and when it doesn't.**
▸ **Ingrain songs into your memory.**
▸ **Make a playlist that is task oriented. Train your brain with your assembled playlist.**
▸ **Look for new and old songs.**
▸ **Use guided imagery.**
▸ **Use a song's BPM to help you organize your playlist.**
▸ **Use your emotional connections to songs.**

Exercise

1. **Assembling Your Playlist.** Pick a variety of tunes that you think heighten your alertness. Listen to identify with specific words of the song and catch that riff that brings with

it an immediately arousing effect. Monitor changes in your heart and breathing rates. You want to notice which of your choices increase those rates most and which make you feel the most alert. As you learn to use this method, you can create a chart to graph the way specific tunes make you feel. Then later you can match songs with your desired results and compare their effectiveness.

Program your selections for a specific activity—anything from your drive to or from work, your lunch break, or a time before your next office meeting, important call, or athletic activity. Arc your list to a specific effect you are after: arrange your choices from high alert to highest alert, and place a slower, feel-good tune at the end to help you cool down or balance your great mind-set.

Playlist Bonus

Combine BPM with an advanced meditation practice. Arc your playlist so that your first tracks are at or less than 100 BPM and then your next plays elevate to 120 or 130. You can alternate a seven- to ten-minute span of lower-BPM music with one to three minutes of higher-BPM music. For guided imagery, try to visualize yourself playing on a field of green grass or walking in a fragrant garden with a bright sunrise and birds noisily waking and hopping from branch to branch in the trees, setting yourself up nicely for feelings of contentment, relaxation, and joy as you plan your day and go about your tasks. Here you are using BPM and meditation to get you simultaneously highly alert and balanced.

Chapter 5

HOW TO USE MUSIC TO FEEL HAPPIER

Music produces a kind of pleasure
which human nature cannot do without.

—Confucius

Why does music drive us to joy, bliss, and ecstasy? And how can we use those reactions in our brain to our advantage?

Freud coined the term PLEASURE PRINCIPLE in 1911; it means that people seek pleasure and avoid pain. Sigmund Freud claimed that we primarily target our attention early in life toward satisfying physical and emotional needs. For example, it is common for young children to express themselves emotionally regardless of the consequences. Likewise, it is common for children out shopping with their parents to "want" their mom or dad to purchase a certain item that has caught their attention, no matter what, even though the product may be of inferior quality, and despite the parents' offer to buy the same thing, but of higher quality, elsewhere. As we all mature, however, Freud believed that most of us learn to override such immediate urges for options that will prove more favorable in the long term. Nevertheless, he insisted that, despite our ability to override instant gratification, we still try to experience pleasure when the opportunity arises—and sometimes when it is inappropriate.

Today, as we peer into the brain with instruments that Freud could only imagine a hundred years ago, we understand that our perceptions, actions, and recurring behaviors are linked through a complex array of chemical processes and electrical circuits that provide the framework for how we individually deal with pain and pleasure. Science today proves what Freud suspected: our brain is indeed wired to sway us toward the greatest reward.

Your brain doesn't always, however, sway you toward the reward that will bring you the best result in the long term, say, working hard to get the promotion you want at work. Sometimes you'll choose to crash on the couch late at night instead of putting in a few more hours on that project your boss is waiting for, going for the immediate reward of blissful vegging out. So this drive to seek reward has both advantages and disadvantages. It's great, for example, when we are able to balance our desires with our responsibilities and social mores, and those then safely lead us to get what we need, what we want, and what's best out of life. But seeking reward may not be so good when it vaults us away from our goals and toward destructive behaviors—sometimes in just a matter of seconds. Reward, in terms of brain science, is more than just a philosophical concept. Reward is philosophical, psychological, and physiological all at the same time.

One thing that makes humans different from all other creatures is our ability to create a total fiction in our mind (an imagined scenario) and use that scene to parallel what we want to happen (in real life), seeing what works and what doesn't in terms of our goals and then ultimately making a decision. This uniquely human capacity is based in our brain's attention network, which relies on information we have stored in memory, external information that is available to us, and how we gather this information together to find a solution to things.

For example, say you put a rat in a box. And say there is a green light and a lever in the front of the box (in psychology this is known as the SKINNER BOX, named after the behavioral psychologist B. F. Skinner). If the rat pushes the lever when the green light goes on, it gets fed Purina Rat Chow (there really is such a thing). You can train a rat to do this. Now let's put me into a similar box, except let's reward me with hundred-dollar bills instead of rat chow. I push the lever a thousand times and make $100,000. Then one day you tell me that you are going to put a red light in the box. You also tell me that if the red light goes on, a lethal electrical shock will be administered through the lever. When I see the red light go on, no matter if I want the hundred-dollar bill or not, I will imagine (create a fiction in my head) what will happen, and I will "choose" to stay away from the lever. The rat, however, having been rewarded with rat chow one thousand times will see the red light go on and go for the Purina. But don't feel bad for rats. They generally do well living conditioned lives. Humans, however, enjoy choice.

We, as opposed to rats and other creatures, can attend imagined scenarios and have feelings and thoughts about them, can consider a variety of outcomes, and can then make a decision on how we want things to go. Thinking helps you get the job done. It helps you connect what happens in your environment to you and your desires. It helps you make choices and feel in control.

—Joseph

Normally, as we move through our daily routines, we become conditioned to pay attention to what will reward us and to veer away from what will not. We put more focus on information that we believe can help us predict or acquire reward (down the line) than on information that we think does not. Remember that this is all based on what we expect our reality to be, and our reality is biased by how all our neurotransmitters work together with our body to maintain a stable level of wellness.

Matching Your Goals to Pleasure

As we discussed earlier, dopamine is the brain's self-produced pleasure drug. Dopamine balance is also a key factor in maintaining the fine line between appropriate pleasure-seeking behavior and that which crosses the line and may not be in our best interests. In terms of daily goals, it is the anticipation of a pleasurable event that releases dopamine into specific pathways in the brain, which in turn motivates you to get what you want while avoiding what you fear, like pain, getting hurt, getting caught, and the like. And this, again, can be good or bad.

A constant balance is needed for us to appropriately process information, to perceive reality, and to carry out the decisions that guide our many daily actions needed to accomplish our personal long-term goals. Looking through the zoom lens of evolution, dopamine orients us—in a primordial way—to move through our environment, always with an air of anticipation, as we attempt to maintain our social composure and relate with the world around us, but always while looking for pleasure and minimizing pain.

So what's happening is that your brain is rewarding you (or not) all day long for doing what you perceive brings you happiness. The reward and pleasure you feel train you to use that same solution the next time—again, it could be good or bad. The tricky part is in the perception, because, of course, our take on things can be less than accurate. In the example of the child who wants her parents to buy her something at the store, satisfying that immediate urge can make the child feel happy.

But consider what training that behavior can lead to.

Getting Happier: A Case Study

Imagine, for example, an individual who has an upcoming speech he must deliver in front of an auditorium filled with colleagues. He is up for a promotion very soon, and he would really like to get it. His boss has asked him to present a new product description to his colleagues. The product is something that the boss would like to acquire because she feels that it is important to the company's portfolio. She has informed him that she will need his colleagues' support, however, before she can purchase the product. In addition, she expects some resistance from his coworkers. In short, his pitch could make or break her goal. He feels that it is going to be a hard sell, but if he can pull it off successfully, he will be in a great position for the promotion he wants.

He is nervous, however, about the potential resistance. His first impulse is to give a short speech, although he'd like it even better if he could get out of it. Just the thought of getting out of the presentation gets his dopamine flowing—it would be so easy to follow this path of thinking and avoid the source of his fears. Again, thinking about avoiding the presentation rewards him even further. But he can see where these thoughts are headed, and they are not in his best interest. He is not living in a box; nor is he a slave to the chemicals and sparks in his head. He can create options, override urges, and exercise choice.

The first thing he wants to do is get over his fears, get himself feeling good and motivated and flowing. He can do this by stimulating his dopamine production and cutting it off at just the right time. This is where his playlist can help.

Let's imagine he has a playlist titled "Euphoria." This playlist has one purpose: to get his dopamine flying. His "Euphoria" playlist includes two tracks that are his all-time favorites. Having taken them from the top of his lists, he knows that the two songs can influence his dopamine level—they always make him feel good. The first track is "Everlong," by the Foo Fighters, which has a BPM of 152. He uses it to train his brain out of rewarding him for avoiding challenges that he knows are important for him to face head-on. This song works because it sends him flying into a powerful and fearless flow. The operative word here, for him, is *fearless*. He absolutely loves the band and especially this song.

He has already trained himself to anticipate the fat, distorted power chords, which make him feel invincible. He especially anticipates a section in the song when the music stops completely for a moment and then comes in with the power chords he loves and the grungy but beautifully melodic vocals singing the chorus—"Hello / I've waited for you / Everlong"—the perfect mix for how he wants to feel, strong, quick-thinking, and fluid.

He visualizes himself in a fictional setting, effortlessly fighting for his life and defeating all kinds of imaginary assailants that come in his path. He anticipates the line, "Breathe out / So I can breathe you in" because he does both when he hears this line; he breathes out and breathes in and lets the music flow through him head to toe. He anticipates the song having an empowering effect on him, and his anticipation drives his dopamine production up ever further. All he has to do now is press play.

The next song he has on his playlist is "So Long Astoria" by the Ataris. For him, it is the thick, distorted guitar playing again and the song's 183 BPM that does it for him. He anticipates the crisp, snapping, warp-speed drum hits and raspy, melodic vocals jetting over them. He also anticipates the line, "Life is only as good as the memories we make." He sings it in his head as he hears it. The line becomes a sort of mantra for him, a chant. The mix of music, his own voice, his expectations, and the song's message help him synchronize the way he feels physically and mentally to the song's powerful output and summon more positive energy from himself to get the job done.

Both songs make him feel unshakable and strong. He repeats them until he has driven away any fear and his mind is flowing right where he wants it: ready to meet the challenge. He knows he is there when he has become oblivious to any fears regarding the presentation, and his demeanor is light, quick, happy, and flowing. He is not even thinking about the text of his presentation because he is confident about it, knows he will know it, and is energized and anticipating doing a bang-up job. He anticipates the reward of people liking it and giving his boss the support she wants, thus putting himself in the best place for promotion. Knowing all this further drives his dopamine production and strengthens his performance all the more.

Here's why: when your brain gets what it wants, the cascade of dopamine immediately causes feelings of bliss and happiness that typically trigger motor actions like smiling and laughter. In terms of focus, we know that dopamine can influence what details you pay attention to. You go for those that reward you more. So by feeling motivated and confident and by anticipating being in a better place for promotion, he will pay even closer attention to the right detail—reading the audience more accurately, not shying away from tough questions he expects, better distinguishing between what is relevant and irrelevant, and providing better arguments, forcefully yet fluidly. Plus, he will look and be stronger and happier.

When Dopamine Levels Drop

It is good to be aware that when dopamine levels drop, you feel a drop in pleasure. This aspect of dopamine plays a role in addiction and in compulsive behaviors, when the feelings that a typical release of the hormone brought on no longer bring the same level of pleasure, and it wears off sooner than expected. When this happens, your need for larger and more frequent doses of the hormone can drive thoughts and behaviors to inappropriate and even dangerous places—like a person who after hearing disappointing news compulsively cracks an out-of-place joke to get himself laughing and feeling better. Or the dieter who has a bad day at work and then has an increased desire for comfort foods that are supposed to be off his menu. Or the heroin addict who has come to crave the rush of pleasure he feels upon the first sight of his needle before ever injecting the drug into his bloodstream.

Sometimes when something turns out better than expected, you experience a surge in dopamine release. This sends you into a high, feel-good mood, but then when the effect wears off, you drop back down. Now, just like the person whose dopamine levels were low to begin with, you too are out looking for reward to make you feel good again.

The tricky part is that in addition to paying out rewards, dopamine plays a major role in orchestrating what you consider something you should pay attention to—both internally and externally. So when your levels drop, it is easy to sway your attention to things with more immediate payoffs, whether or not those things are good for you (and your goals). This is a possible reason some people who experience some form of overnight sensation, like winning an influential award or a large sum of money or receiving a larger raise than they expected—sometimes display careless judgment shortly after.

A typical example is all the dangerous drinking and driving that can accompany the celebration of such events. Attention swerves toward what will bring the quickest pleasure rather than what is best or most sensible at the moment. So it is important to remind yourself that dropping levels of dopamine can influence your thoughts, how you participate in work and family events, and even your dreams.

You can, however, use your playlist to help you compensate as the hormone dips downward. The following are some sample playlists that others have used according to their needs and tastes. Notice that in each of the playlists the songs tend to increase in intensity. What's most important is that the users like the songs a lot and feel spikes in pleasure from them. You can play your playlists straight through, or you can play individual tracks as needed and match them to specific situations.

Sample "Euphoria" Playlist No. 1

▸ **"Thunder Road,"** Bruce Springsteen

▸ **"Won't Get Fooled Again,"** The Who

▸ **"Round About,"** Yes

▸ **"Layla,"** Derek and the Dominos

▸ **"Brown Sugar,"** The Rolling Stones

Sample "Euphoria" Playlist No. 2

▶ **"Billie Jean,"** Michael Jackson

▶ **"(I've Had) The Time of My Life,"** Bill Medley and Jennifer Warnes (on the *Dirty Dancing* soundtrack)

▶ **"Respect,"** Aretha Franklin

▶ **"Dance to the Music,"** Sly and the Family Stone

▶ **"I Want to Take You Higher,"** Ike and Tina Turner

Sample "Euphoria" Playlist No. 3

▶ **"Punk Rock Girl,"** The Dead Milkmen

▶ **"Karma Chameleon,"** Sixpack

▶ **"Mrs. Robinson,"** The Lemonheads

▶ **"I Fought the Law,"** Green Day

▶ **"Rise Above,"** Black Flag

▸▸ The septal nuclei (also connected with the nucleus accumbens) is the one site in the brain responsible for the experience of physical pleasure, and stimulating it electrically brings about orgasm. There is an interesting story that makes its way around the "neuro" world, involving a series of experiments done in psychiatric institutes in Canada. In these experiments, patients were implanted with small stimulating electrodes in the septal nuclei and given a button that would let them control the shocks to their brain, almost instantly bringing them to orgasm. The stimulation worked for both men and women, although there were clear differences based on gender in the reactions of patients.

For the men, self-stimulation occurred intermittently with extended periods between stimulating events because of ejaculation, which is an integral part of the process of orgasm. However, for the women tested in these studies, there were no such physical restrictions on the duration of orgasm—one patient in particular was found to have orgasms extending for more than two hours nonstop. In cases like these, patients were willing and able to continue self-stimulating at the cost of all other drives, including the drive to eat. Needless to say, the O switch and electrodes had to be removed before the patients could return to their routine patterns of behavior.

—Don

Staying Balanced When It's Not Easy

Our craving for a dopamine fix is at the core of our most basic motivations and drives for food, sex, and shelter from the elements (not necessarily in that order). Hence, we experience immediate feelings of pleasure and satisfaction when we succeed at appeasing these drives, and then our memory circuits are updated so we don't forget. This is nature's way of sustaining us, both physically and mentally, for the long-term. But sometimes the drives discombobulate us, and no amount of self-talk can prevent us from doing, saying, and feeling things we know are wrong—but we just can't stop.

Here's where chemical balances in your reward and emotional networks come into play. You don't want your drive for pleasure to become a need that overpowers all your other drives—like the child who cannot reason or the cat or dog that jets across a highway to chase a squirrel. Remember the lesson of the Skinner box. This imbalance is what happens in the brain of drug addicts, where the most rewarded networks and interconnections dominate, driving the single-minded thought processes and behaviors of the abuser away from normal brain patterns.

The Strength of Serotonin

Let's look at another self-produced brain drug that helps you balance the effects of dopamine and that can be influenced by the music you listen to: SEROTONIN, the well-known neurotransmitter associated with regulating mood. Knowing something about the mechanics of your brain functions and how music influences them can be as powerful as going to therapy or taking prescription drugs.

We know that serotonin production, somewhat in contrast to dopamine, can and does involve the higher-order thinking processes of your mind. It affects your mood and influences your goal-directed behaviors. Serotonin helps you reason things out when you need to and respond to things emotionally. It helps you empathize and focus and stay in flow. We also know that music you perceive as pleasant increases serotonin levels in your blood. This makes it a useful tool in balancing the effects of dopamine by helping you power up drives and behaviors that will help you avoid losing sight of your goals and instead bring your optimized, flowing mind to bear on them.

For example, if you are hungry enough, you will feel a sense of reward (again reinforced with dopamine) by simply getting food—any food—into you. In terms of evolution, primitive instinct tells us that you need food to stay alive. There's no time to get particular when you need to eat, as long as the food is not poisonous.

However, once the basic food drive is met, higher-order cognitive processes get involved (those affected by serotonin and rewarded by dopamine), in which you are able to remember and learn about which foods offer the most health benefits. This information helps you choose to seek those foods that taste better and that carry increased nutrients—thus feeling happy and being rewarded at a higher level than if you had just found some raw grains to alleviate your hunger. In this way, your brain's reward mechanisms, at both primitive and cognitive levels, allow you to prefer specific goals that bring you the most reward—like eating healthier and tastier foods—and to hone the skills necessary to find the best foods and gain the greatest benefits.

It's this higher-level information processing, memory, learning, perception, motivation, and reward that work together to attain the most pleasure out of life as possible. These combined and coordinated brain systems help you maintain balance and achieve optimum-level performance in whatever you do. It's your job, however, to use your thinking, higher-level brain to make wise choices that keep your pleasure circuits in check.

What We Can Learn from Reading and Dopamine

Before we dive back into talking about music, a little discussion about how your brain's reward mechanism connects to other things, such as enjoyable reading, may help. Seeing how this connection works may further clarify music's effects on the same circuits and how you can use your playlist to drive them.

You already know that your enthusiasm for reading, even for a certain type of book or magazine, can be simply for the pleasure it gives you. So let's take a closer look at what happens when you are reading for such a reward.

As soon as some of us start thinking about a book we want to read, our brain triggers the release of dopamine into our bloodstream. It might take as little as seeing an ad for a new book by your favorite author that makes you instantly anticipate the pleasure you will garner from reading it.

Then, once you decide to purchase the book, just getting to where you can buy it puts your brain into overdrive. All this anticipation starts physiological processes throughout your body, including the release of dopamine. Your motivation to read your new book keeps heightening until you finally sit down and crack open the pages. Then, as long as the text meets your expectations, it will bring forth a rush of comfort, joy, satisfaction, and a whole range of other pleasurable feelings.

Now let's change the scenario a little bit. Let's go to a wife who is trying to make peace with her mother-in-law—with whom she has had a falling out. The problem is that nothing she has tried has helped. In fact, her mother-in-law's resistance to making peace with her has in many ways left her more irritated. So she decides to go to her favorite bookstore and see what books are available that can offer some tips about making peace with family members. She discovers several that look good to her. One appeals to her more than the others because it seems most suited to her situation.

Now, every step she takes, from purchasing the book to driving home in anticipation of being able to start reading the book, is rewarded. She feels a sense of further reward anticipating that the information she gets from the book will help fix her relationship with her mother-in-law.

A week or so later she tries out a new approach at bridging the gap with her mother-in-law. What she discovers is that the book she powered up with actually helped her create a successful dialogue with her mother-in-law and got their relationship moving in a better, more peaceful direction. She feels rewarded as a result and again as her mother-in-law's attitude toward her warms up.

The next time she has a life issue she needs information to help resolve, she is already predisposed to start looking for book help. It worked so well with her mother-in-law, that just thinking about doing a search to see what available resources are out there for other issues begins to make her feel rewarded. The more she follows this procedure for getting helpful information when she needs it, the more pleasure she takes not only in reading but also in every other step of the process. Her pleasure ripples out beyond just book reading and into the whole chain of components that, for her, leads to successful behavior. If she attends a seminar and someone mentions a helpful book, she writes it down and feels a sense of reward at doing even that. She might, at times, even look for seminars and discussions with self-improvement as the topic, and she starts to feel a sense of excitement and reward at that juncture.

A major change in her happiness is that it is becoming more process oriented than outcome oriented. Because of that, she is in a flow mind-set more often and for longer periods of time. This accomplishment—beginning to live in and crave living in flow—then reinforces all her actions, brightens her mood, and makes her mind happy and flowing for longer periods of time. She rewards herself further for making these choices, and she commits them to memory for the next time.

At this point she is feeling rewarded not only because she is reading books but also because she is linking everything in the process with her successes and the satisfying mind-set that brings along with it, rather than reading just as a diversion or to kill time—although reading, for her, still is that too.

Understanding how your reward systems work, their tie-in

to planning, anticipation, action, and ultimately the receipt of reward, sets the stage for how you can use your playlist to increase your dopamine levels and optimize your pleasure, to make you happy and keep you flowing.

In all cases, whether we are talking about reading or tunes on your playlist, it's the melding of your thoughts and actions with your body that regulates and lets loose the pleasurable sensations and happiness you feel from accomplishing a rewarding task. In terms of music, just as with reading, you can feel rewarded in each stage of the process that leads to your satisfaction and happiness: learning about how music affects you brain and body, finding the right tunes to help you, practicing and experimenting with them, buying an iPod or MP3 player, making various playlists, specializing playlists for targeted goals, reaping the benefits, and becoming happy. This awareness will ultimately train your brain to seek happiness as a state of mind and to reward itself for doing so and for keeping you there—in flow.

If you feel pleasure from listening to a piece of music, then it's possible for you to use music as a tool to drive your reward system to increase its dopamine output, thus leading you to increased feelings of comfort, satisfaction, and happiness in very specifically targeted situations. With a little training and practice, it's possible to get your brain to automatically start sending instructions throughout your mind and body to reward those feelings intrinsically. Ultimately, they will become both your goal and your reward. Philosophically, psychologically, and physiologically speaking, you can be living in flow.

Precautions

You might be wondering if it is possible to rely on a piece of music too much. The answer is that you can. When this happens, you run the risk of diluting that song's potential effects. For this reason, we always recommend continuously updating and adding to your playlist so that you won't exhaust it.

Balance should always weigh in too. For example, if your brain is flying on frequent dopamine highs, it can become dissatisfied and require higher levels of the hormone to reach the same highs, even though it is already at higher-than-average production.

This is what happens when you have just had your perfect-ten day—the best ever—and the next day is a seven. Even if your usual day is a five—with the seven technically better—it is common to feel a little down or like you are operating with less focus or energy. What you are feeling is lower levels of dopamine. Even though your production is a little higher than usual, it is still lower than the day before. If you are hit with the perfect dud of a day after a perfect ten, you may experience even less pleasure, motivation, and focus in general. Some of us may remember those days after an exam—say, after your last finals—when you feel somewhat scattered, as though you have lost something and cannot find it. But what you really lost was that surge of stimulating neurochemicals, mostly dopamine, which kept you going no matter what.

If you push your dopamine and the other neurochemicals to an imbalanced state, your happiness and flow will deteriorate. Excessive dopamine production can fuel feelings of paranoia and an inability to tell what is important from what is not. So again, it's important not to overdo it.

▸▸ I recently gave my daughters (six and four years old) my iPod, and let them play with it around the house. As it turned out, I discovered another way to attach more pleasure to old songs. They loved scrolling through it and finding songs on my playlists that they personally loved. At times, we would share the earphones; I'd take one and either Isabella or Veronica the other. Sometimes they shared earphones. Then one day while heading to the college, I turned on my iPod and my usual playlist wasn't playing. For a moment I wasn't sure why but then remembered my daughters playing their favorite songs. The iPod scramble was responding to their selections. "How great!"

I thought as I then began to visualize each daughter traversing the house, earphones on and dancing to the tunes. I was able to hear their favorite tunes, the ones they played over and over. What a great feel-good memory we made.

As I said, it attached new pleasure to old songs. I can now play those tunes and relive my memories of my daughters listening to them as a special treat when I need charging as I work in my office. I turn on my iPod, take a look at some photos of the girls on my wall, and enjoy the good vibes. Sometimes it's just what I need to keep me happy. I encourage you to try something similar with your friends, family, partners, and children.

—Joseph

Putting Together Your Playlist

Here is how to begin choosing songs for a playlist that will help increase your happiness.

▸ **First, pick songs you like a lot.**

> ‣ Pay attention to when a certain song works and when it doesn't.
> ‣ Ingrain songs into your memory.
> ‣ Make a playlist that is task oriented. Train your brain with your assembled playlist.
> ‣ Look for new and old songs.
> ‣ Use guided imagery.
> ‣ Use a song's BPM to help you organize your playlist.
> ‣ Use your emotional connections to songs.
> ‣ Use your brain's reward system.

Exercise

1. **When Security Pleases.** Pick a short tune that is an old favorite. Begin playing it a few times in the morning and again in the afternoon or evening. It doesn't matter if your tune is an instrumental or has lyrics. What matters is that you associate your music with feelings of security. First, think about what *security* means to you and what impressions those thoughts bring to mind. Identify the one that really makes you feel the best when you think about it, like an old memory of being close with your mom, dad, or someone who would give you that sense of security when you felt really safe. Now actively listen to your music. As you listen to the song a few times, pick out a segment that you really enjoy and focus on your immediate feelings, both in your mind and in your body. Play the song again, and anticipate that upcoming segment and try to

pair it with the image of safety you identified and with the expectation that your feelings of safety will intensify and last longer each time you hear it. Practicing with this music will reinforce the anticipation and feelings of security and comfort. Try to recognize what sounds and words (as well as other images that come to mind) are responsible for increasing your positive experience. Try to learn and remember those cues so you can increase the effect over time. This will take you to, and reinforce, the next level of satisfaction; that is, feeling happy in simply seeking information can lead you to a feeling of reward. Add your musical choices to your playlist.

2. **When Calm Pleases.** Whether you are trying to calm yourself down or crank up your attention and focus, succeeding at the task can be a pleasurable event, and any positive feelings will reward your attempt at changing your brain. That way, the more you practice, the greater is your reward. What's good about this is that you are ultimately training your brain to start instructing itself—automatically—to get you happy. Your job is to use your playlist to help get you there. Start by looking over your playlist and picking out a couple of possibilities for driving your brain in your desired state. Let's say you want to calm down after a long and stressful day at work. If so, then listen to a few of your choices and pick out the one that gives you the feeling that's closest to your goal. It's easier than you think.

    For instance, one individual we know listens to the Foo Fighters' "Virginia Moon" when he wants to calm down and relax his mood and stress level. He likes the song's relatively slow beat and its style, as well as its blend of the harmonies in the musical arrangement. But ultimately, he says, it's really all about the words. The words bring images into his mind. And he has control of the images and feelings he wants to focus on. In addition, the words of "Virginia Moon" have special meaning to him because he lives in Virginia and because he can easily imagine himself walking on a beach in the moonlight to feel calmer as he listens to the song. He puts his focus on feeling the rhythm and anticipating the tune's lyrics and changes.

As we have said, the use of imagery with music can amplify a song's ability to influence your brain waves so that they suit your immediate needs. By thinking about calming things, you will feel calmer. And remember, you can reinforce this effect further by remembering to breathe slowly and deeply as you listen to your chosen tune with the goal of slowing your heartbeat and relaxing your body. By doing all these things while listening to your playlist, you will bring yourself the happiness you've sought and face the day's next events in a state of flow.

3. **When Excitement Pleases.** By changing the music and the mental imagery it evokes, you can excite your brain to release serotonin and dopamine, increase your heart and breathing rates to influence a state of physical readiness, and ultimately change your thought processes to focus on your goal of being pumped up. So, in this case, you definitely don't want the previously mentioned slow beat from "Virginia Moon." Instead, you might pick another Foo Fighters song, say, something like "Best of You," or

maybe something by Sick Puppies, like "Street Fighter (War)"—both songs are relatively up-tempo but still not too extreme in their pace; they are middle of the road. The key is to get yourself into synch with the beat of the drums and to focus on how they build up along with the increasing sound of the guitar and bass. Let your imagination create actions in your mind that will pump you up—you don't want to be sitting on a nice beach; you want to be flying, racing, or fighting. Imagine the exact state of mind you want to be in. Think about getting up and moving around if there's room or even singing along to activate your entire body. Again, try to find lyrics in your songs that have powerful meaning to you, and use those to drive your brain's circuits. The songs "Street Fighter (War)" and "Best of You" convey a defiant tone in their lyrics. The use of defiant words in these songs can help you build up strong emotions. It's an excellent way to excite your senses and get energized and motivated, which are both rewarding and pleasurable.

Chapter 6

HOW MUSIC CAN ORGANIZE YOUR BRAIN

*Playing scales is like a boxer skipping
rope or punching a bag.
It's not the thing in itself; it's
preparatory to the activity.*

—Jazz guitarist Barney Kessel

Picture this: It's 8:30 a.m. You arrived at the airport an hour and a half ago, having left home very early this morning. In the last hour you've picked up your baggage and rental car, gotten directions to your hotel, and driven yourself there. Now you're outside the conference room door, and you have ten minutes, at most, to update your slides and mentally prepare yourself to run through a briefly adjusted presentation. At 9 a.m. you will be speaking in one of the hotel's larger conference rooms to an audience of more than 250 experts in your field.

You usually try to schedule such trips so you arrive the night before—to organize your thoughts and chill out a little—but this time there was simply too much to do at the office that couldn't wait for your return. Then, at the last minute before leaving home, you received new information that you have to include in your presentation, and you still have to deal with that. You are having a hard time getting organized. You don't know where to begin and are feeling stressed out and somewhat overwhelmed.

You may not have had this exact experience, but you've surely been in a similar situation in which you felt over-aroused, anxious, stressed out, and disorganized. When you are like this, your brain tries to lighten your load by moving into a state of reduced arousal. The problem, however, is that by doing this you have lower mental sharpness and ability.

We all have an ideal brain activity pattern (BAP) that is linked to our peak mental functioning—flow. And when we are tired, stressed, and not totally with it, as may be the case in a high-pressure environment like the conference room, which requires increased attention, focus, and concentration for long periods, you are more likely to be out of flow than in it, and your BAP would parallel that. This is mostly because your brain activity in such cases is dominated by your emotions and by your level of arousal, which would likely be in the stress zone.

When you are tired and/or stressed and out of flow, your BAP reorganizes into a new pattern that is away from its highest-functioning state.

This new pattern is less optimal and possibly even dysfunctional. Here is the thing: the longer your BAP stays in a less optimal state, the more likely your brain is to rewire itself to that state (remember plasticity), and ultimately this less optimal mind-set will become your modus operandi. In a way, when this happens, you are training your brain for disorganization.

It is possible to use your playlist to get out of that kind of spiral. Music can facilitate more organized and clearer thinking, and as such, it can improve your ability to perform at a very high level. It is a powerful intervention for disorganized brain activity, and when combined with the organizational power of imagery and meaningful interpretation of lyrics, it is possible to use it to drive key brain systems that facilitate a stable state of improved focus and organization. You can, by hitting a few plays, redirect your less optimal BAP and reinforce (reward) any improved patterns that replace old dysfunctional ones.

Playlist Bonus

Start with those natural sounds we're all exposed to: water flowing, nice and calming rhythms of an ocean breeze. Close your eyes and imagine ocean waves. You will activate a location in your brain's temporal lobes that allows you to see the sound as you listen and imagine this scenery. Think about the colors of both the ocean and sky, about the soft blue-green hues. Think about scents as well, the salty breeze and smell of warm sand—maybe sunscreen lotion—however you imagine it. Try to stay with this for about five to ten minutes. It doesn't matter where you are or whether you're in flow; you can use this image to put your brain in an organizational mode. Once you open your eyes and proceed with your next task, you will feel refreshed, but you will also find it easier to organize your thinking and activities. This is not a panacea but a tool that can help you jump-start your brain almost anytime, anywhere.

The following are some sample playlists including environmental sounds that others have put on their iPods and MP3 players to supplement the exercise here. Of course, it's best to select tracks according to your own needs and taste.

Sample "Organizing" Playlist No. 1

▸ **"Ocean Waves"**

▸ **"Light Waves"**

▸ **"Stream with Bird Sounds"**

▸ **"Waterfalls"**

▸ **"Distant Thunder"**

Sample "Organizing" Playlist No. 2

▸ **"Campfire Night"**

▸ **"Desert Wildlife at Night"**

▸ **"Loons"**

▸ **"Sands and Seagulls"**

▸ **"Wolves"**

Power Up with Musical Metaphors

When you are listening to a piece of music, you are in part, experiencing—through sound—that composer's (or player's) state of mind in the world. You are legitimately in that person's mind. This is great because it gives you access to that person's mind to help you enhance your life. What makes this possible is that your brain is naturally wired for EMPATHY. And empathy plays a major role in our ability to experience the life of another person through mixes and matches of what we see, hear, smell, taste, touch, and understand. But its effects don't stop there.

When we take our understandings from one walk of life or experience and bring them to bear on other experiences (our own or others) from other areas of life, we are creating metaphor. Metaphors help us improve our reactions to the world around us. They do this by deepening our understandings and feelings about things and helping us better organize what we think and do. The better your empathy, the better equipped you are to see and apply metaphor. Together these skills help make us more sensitive and, as a result, better able to strategize our goals and problem solve our lives. What's more, they help us understand how others organize and problem solve their lives. Empathy and metaphor are essential tools for accomplishing just about everything we do.

The more you practice empathy, the better you get at it.

Music can help you get the practice you need to train more of each of these tools into your brain. For example, you might start by identifying with a singer you like and think, "That person sounds like me." You may be referring to his or her lyrics or tone. Yet as you listen even closer, you enter the next stage of listening, in which you can identify more clearly, "This is where my head would be at; this is what I would feel in his or her space." Here you see what your perspective in the same scenario might be. And with the next stage of listening, you can identify, "This is what things mean to the singer in this space, how it feels to the singer." Now you are seeing and feeling through the singer's mind.

Later, with a little reflection, you can compare where your head went in the song to where the singer's mind was. Now you have two perspectives: yours and the singer's. And both can be useful to you and your life.

Consider the following tunes. Let's start with Metallica's "Master of Puppets," viewed as one of the best heavy thrash-metal songs ever. The song presents mostly the raw wails (instrumental and voice) of the "master." His tone, as well as the instrumental's tone, is heavy. It basically says and conveys an image of attitude that belts out, "!@/#$% you!" What's interesting is that the song is arranged so that you don't immediately know who the "master" refers to. It's your call for a while. But during this time, the song's intensely dark sounds conjure Faustian images of demons in your head. And by about a third of the way through the tune, most listeners have figured out that the "master" is any one of a number of addictive drugs—cocaine, heroin, meth. These are the demons.

Then a second voice is brought into the song. This voice "sounds" like the desperate voice of the creature, who, in the song, the master ravages and mocks. You quickly realize that the creature is indeed the addict, and he (or she) is totally subservient to the master. The master shows no mercy in dominating its creation, to the point of destroying all of his or her dreams. At this point in the song's metaphor, you realize that you have been listening to one of the most dramatic anti-drug songs ever recorded.

That said, you can take the metaphor of master and creature, drug and addict, and apply it beyond the scope of the song—wherever in your life you feel you are or have been enslaved. The message of the metaphor is to get yourself out of enslavement and recapture your own, true identity, and ultimately to save your dreams. The song's energy, similar to a ride in a rocket ship, is intended to spark an epiphany in the addicted listener that energizes the transformation away from drug use and into a healthier life. The intended audience who might actually benefit from the message would need to recognize the meaning of the lyrics to their life and then use the strong emotional connection to the music to help in their battle to pull themselves out of the quicksand. However, you don't have to be addicted to a substance to grab onto the song's power. You can use its energy to organize and get yourself unstuck from anything once you apply it metaphorically.

Now, let's go to the other side of the musical spectrum. Imagine Enya's megahit "Caribbean Blue." The difference in energy and imagery that this tune sparks is immediately apparent and felt. From the song's first soothing lines—"So the world goes round and round with all you ever knew"—and its repeating looped synth sounds, you are invited into a slow, hypnotic, meditative mind-set that is the music's core energy. You can imagine the vast, deep blueness of Caribbean skies, tinted with shades of rose and white, and the refreshing, calming sway of waves rolling over rock formations into long, warm strands of shoreline. You can imagine an environment of beautifully plush flowers open and bright along the moist earth, or a flock of slow-sailing birds floating along the skyline with endless water beneath them and shining blue sky above. As you meditate on these images, you can feel your physiology changing, your breathing slowing down and deepening, your muscles relaxing, and your heart rate slowing. You can also feel the overall influence of the song getting stronger. What you don't feel is that it is grooving deeper into your memory. This will train your brain to move out of overdrive and into a more optimal BAP—whenever you need to organize or whenever you are overaroused.

The following are two sample playlists that will help you get organized for real-life situations.

Sample "Organizing for Work Projects" Playlist

▸ **"Back on the Chain Gang,"** The Pretenders

▸ **"Let's Work,"** Mick Jagger

▸ **"Taking Care of Business,"** Bachman-Turner Overdrive

▸ **"Finest Worksong,"** R.E.M.

▸ **"She Works Hard for the Money,"** Donna Summer

Sample "Organizing for Family Projects" Playlist

▶ **"Heigh-Ho,"** Snow White and the Seven Dwarfs

....

▶ **"Notre Dame Fight Song"**

....

▶ **"Chicago Bulls Intro Theme"**

....

▶ **"This Land Is Your Land,"** Los Lobos/Grateful Dead

....

▶ **"Rock Around the Clock,"** Bill Haley

....

Organize with Rhythm

Rhythm is characterized as a pattern of beats in speech or verse. The brain is made up of many small electrical generators scattered in key areas, and it uses rhythm to synchronize the activity of those generators, activity that spreads through their connections to other regions of the brain. Managing the communication among all these generators (like beating drums signaling from one group to another) is an essential element in how, for instance, your frontal lobes coordinate the thoughts and actions that you need to perform a task, like watching a television program and understanding the plot enough to talk about it at work the next day with your friends. To do this, your frontal lobes have to keep out all the distractions and keep you focused during the program. We can measure brain waves in response to the thoughts generated in the frontal lobes, as well as the connections from the frontal lobes to other parts of the brain. In all cases, the electrical activity in an electroencephalograph (or EEG, which measures your brain waves) tells us about the power in certain locations and the communication taking place between different locations.

Our brain-wave pattern (BWP) is expressed in a relatively narrow range of frequencies (from 0 to 100 Hertz), typically measured from a small number of locations over the scalp surface (from 4 to 250 sites). The frequency patterns that your brain produces on a regular basis are rhythmic in nature and are made from several different generators, most of them deep in the brain.

We can display brain-wave frequency patterns using color-coded maps that tell us how active the various parts of the brain are. These frequency maps and graphs of interconnected regions in the brain tell us how the brain is wired together. Each person's BAP is actually very stable over time (periods of years in adults).

Because brain patterns are so stable, we can collect data from hundreds of people and analyze them to understand what are "NORMAL (BRAIN RHYTHMS)" and which ones are "NOT NORMAL (BRAIN RHYTHMS)" or possibly dysfunctional. It is now possible to take a map of your BAP and compare it with a "normal" group of people who are the same age as you to determine whether your brain patterns look the same (statistically).

It's important to remember that your unique BAP is made from your genes and all your life's experience and is therefore highly customized—one of a kind (unless you have an identical twin, whose brain waves would be almost identical).

But there are general rules of thumb on how your brain's networks can interconnect and operate together, which make it possible to tell what's normal from what's not. There are characteristic activities that match up with deviant patterns of thought and behavior (e.g., obsessive-compulsive disorder, bipolar disorder, personality disorder). There's tons of anatomical evidence supporting the idea that your BAP can indicate a specific psychiatric disorder, like schizophrenia, attention deficit/hyperactivity disorder, or autism, because of how the different brain networks operate together—some might be dominant and others nearly shut down. This is done by measuring the difference of your brain waves in comparison with a "normal" group of brain waves.

Here's an example: Bob and Paul are police officers in New York City who both grew up in New Jersey under quite different circumstances. Both Bob and Paul are of equal age, IQ, and financial stability, but Bob grew up on the streets, and Paul grew up in a high-end neighborhood without much conflict, so he was not very comfortable when it came to his job. As a cop, Paul was quite anxious; he tended to drink a bit too much and some might say that he was depressed. Bob, however, was pretty even tempered, easygoing, and happy, even under stressful situations at work. He was always the guy who was cool, calm, and collected.

If you looked at the resting BAPs for Bob and Paul, you'd find they were quite different from each other, particularly in the three main systems of the brain: (1) the DEFAULT MODE (DM), the system that affects your actions, motivation, and mood; 2) the CENTRAL EXECUTIVE (CE), the system that directs your actions and understands consequences; and (3) the SALIENCE NETWORK (SN), the system responsible for things like empathy, social behavior, and making changes to your actions. These three systems interact continuously as you go through your day to regulate your body and govern your actions, mood, and goals. In Bob's case, his cool, calm, and collected demeanor is because his CE is running on all cylinders and keeping the entire brain on track. His SN is also running at peak efficiency. For Bob, he relies on this part of his brain to be able to read and understand the subtle cues that come from suspects, witnesses, and even bystanders at a crime scene, and he must also use his SN to get along with and respond appropriately to his coworkers.

The reason for Bob's level of happiness is that his DM, the system that most influences how he is feeling, is relatively shut down as compared to his other two systems. This situation means that Bob's brain deals with his environment better and is better able to handle the stress of a FIRST RESPONDER's life on the streets dealing with criminals but also having to deal with people who are not criminals. Here, Bob's brain can quickly understand the difference in the situations and is able to turn down his level of aggression so he does not come on too strong in the given circumstances.

The systems in Paul's brain operate quite differently. Rather than his thinking brain being in charge, over time Paul's DM (his stress brain) has taken over command. His body suffers from the overcharge of neurochemicals, his thoughts constantly wander as he ruminates on past events that he has no control over, and he feels miserable all the time. He hates his job and all the horrible people he has to continually deal with, and he really hates Bob, because he is always so upbeat and happy. Paul's way of coping is to drink, which makes it hard for him to sleep and, in turn, negatively affects his job performance. In this case, Paul is somewhat at the mercy of his DM. Without someone or something to reset the balance in Paul's brain, he could easily spin out of control. Without his executive and social systems online, Paul is very likely to respond inappropriately to situations as events unfold. Communication is required among the CE, DM, and SN systems to coordinate actions and achieve a stable state of mind. In this state, it is conceivable that Paul might easily overreact, thus causing injury or undue harm to an innocent party by not correctly processing the events and acting accordingly.

Let's take a look at an example of a gambler to understand how the SN works to influence the other two systems of the brain. Our gambler, playing the game twenty-one, is using a strategy of holding on fifteen and never taking more than four cards, which has been working quite well and she's been winning, a lot. Her mood is good, she's not drinking so she can think straight, and she is able to pick up the expressions and body language from the other players. The dealer is harder to tell, though.

Then the dealer is replaced, the game proceeds, and she continues to win on and off for a few more hands. After a while, she starts to lose, hand after hand. Is it the new dealer? Is it the other players? Is it her strategy? Her DM starts to kick in, and she is feeling anxious. She doesn't like to lose, and that feeling in her gut is no longer from the thrill of winning but the dread of losing. She thinks, "What is going on?" Her CE takes charge and views the table and other players. What's changed? Another hand is dealt; it's a black jack. She wins, and she feels a little better.

In the next hand, she's dealt a six and a four. She takes a hit and it's a four, which makes fourteen. She takes another hit and the card is an ace (one or eleven) that gives her fifteen. She has hit both her strategy criteria, fifteen and four cards—she holds. The dealer turns his cards; there's a queen and a five and he turns over six for twenty-one. She loses! But she could have used that card. If only she had not stuck to her strategy and taken a fifth card, she would have won. Her stomach leaps, her anxiety swells, and she thinks, "I can't keep losing!" Now is when her SN kicks into full gear, when emotional inputs from her DM and the perceptive influences of her CE must be weighed and overcome to change the strategy that had been working but stopped. Confirmed by neuroimaging studies, the SN (with its tie-in to empathy) has to become involved in the process of making a change in betting strategy. This function extends to all aspects of life when our strategy requires an adjustment.

So, it makes good sense for the brain to use rhythm, or more precisely, the combination of rhythms, to coordinate the activities of a bunch of separate but interconnected networks in the brain to find an appropriate state of balance, given the particular needs and drives of any given moment. It's effective and efficient.

The central nervous system manages the connections among the three main systems through a process called

CROSS-FREQUENCY PHASE COUPLING. In this process, fast frequencies ride on top of slower frequencies, and signals are organized to increase and spread a specific pattern of activity within and across networks, which leads to a new stable state. This process of mixing and grouping of frequencies according to their inherent relationships is also at the core of how music is organized in the brain and why it provides such a powerful tool for reorganizing dysfunctional brain activity.

By selecting music with the right characteristics to help your needs, it is possible to change the dynamics within your brain. Doing so rebalances your key systems, reorganizes your BAP to an improved new state, and changes your behavior so that you are more relaxed, more focused, and so on.

So how do you use your playlist to organize with rhythm? In the case of the two police officers described earlier, Bob's playlist would be quite different from Paul's. Bob's might be filled with songs he can use to maintain his level of excitement and to improve the quality of his sleep, particularly when his schedule is disrupted.

Bob's Sample Playlist

▶ **"We Got the Beat,"** The Go-Gos

▶ **"Everyday People,"** Sly and the Family Stone

▶ **"Morning Song,"** Jewel

▸ **"Goodnight, Irene,"** Willie Nelson (night track)

▸ **"Big Joe and Phantom 309,"** Tom Waits (night track)

In contrast to Bob's playlist, Paul's library of brain music will need to be much different, much more powerful, if he is to get out of his funk and reorganize the balance between his thinking and reacting mind. In this case, Paul might want to listen to tracks that will help diminish his ruminations and his negative assessment of his life and of others around him.

Paul's Sample Playlist

▸ **"Right Now,"** Van Halen

▸ **"Higher,"** Creed

▸ **"Back in the High Life,"** Steve Winwood

▸ **"Don't Stop Believing,"** Journey

▸ **"Angel Standing By,"** Jewel

Paul might also want to consider some individual or group counseling to provide the cognitive-behavioral component of his mental reorganization and rebalancing.

Why Our Brain Loves Patterns

The tendency to group elements together is universal and irresistible. In addition, we know that, once you identify a pattern, the entire "unit" of the pattern rather than the individual elements themselves evokes your response. Take a look. Imagine each of the following slashes (represented as /) and Xs as a whack on a snare drum.

/ / / /	XXXX	/ / / /
/ / / /	XXXX	/ / / /
/ / / /	XXXX	/ / / /
/ / / /	XXXX	/ / / /
Pause	Pause	Pause
/ / / /	/ / / /	XXXX
/ / / /	/ / / /	XXXX
/ / / /	/ / / /	XXXX
/ / / /	/ / / /	XXXX
Pause	Pause	Pause

At first, you may count the four slashes in the first line: one, two, three, four. It doesn't take long to figure out that there will be four beats per line. Once you recognize the pattern, you can predict when each line ends and the next begins as well as when each unit (of four lines) begins and ends, by diverting your attention from individual beats to entire units of beat instead.

If this sound pattern indicated the rhythm of a song—the forward slashes referring to verse and the Xs referring to the chorus, you would in short order be able to tell when the chorus comes around without counting at all. Not only that, but you would be able to retain and recall this song's rhythmic pattern faster and easier the next time.

The rhyming quality of lyrics works the same way, only with lyrics, you combine images (visuals), sound, and rhythm. As you process all three, additional brain networks coordinate, and your expectations are triggered and rewarded through resolution, thus amplifying a song's overall organizational influence on your brain. Importantly, it helps put your mind in a state of flow, and that highly aroused and organized mindset will transfer to other imminent goals.

Putting Together Your Playlist

Here is how to begin choosing songs for a playlist to help increase organization in your brain.

▸ **First, pick songs you like a lot.**

▸ **Pay attention to when a certain song works and when it doesn't.**

▸ **Ingrain songs into your memory.**

▸ **Make a playlist that is task oriented. Train your brain with your assembled playlist.**

▸ **Look for new and old songs.**

▸ **Use guided imagery.**

▸ **Use a song's BPM to help you organize your playlist.**

▸ **Use your emotional connections to songs.**

▸ **Use your brain's reward system.**

▸ **Look for songs you can empathize with.** Put together a

playlist of songs that you want to experience from the singer's perspective: pick tunes with a message that feels like it came straight out of your own head. Then, put yourself into the time, place, and event of the song. See how you would experience these yourself. Then, put yourself in the mind of the singer. Experience the event from that person's perspective, not yours. Ask yourself, "What positive information (and metaphors) can I learn from both my and the singer's perspective that I can apply to my own life situations that I am having a tough time organizing in my mind?" Begin a playlist for those situations, such as "Finding a New Job," or "Organizing for Work," or "Organizing for Family Projects."

▸ **Find songs with strong and obvious rhythm.** Put together a playlist of highly rhythmic songs that you like. Listen closely to the rhythm. Try dancing to the rhythm until you feel it in your body. Or try jogging or even doing housework to the songs and feeling the rhythm in your body as you move. Just feel the rhythms with your body as you listen. Take your mind off the song and move to the rhythm. Try to anticipate when the chorus will come around without having to listen to the words or to count lines. Or maybe it's a certain riff you want to anticipate. Doing this may be a little difficult at first, but with just a little patience you can. If you are jogging (or walking), try to anticipate how far ahead you will be when the next chorus comes around. Don't analyze it—just intuit it. Put together a list of songs that you enjoy and can practice this skill with. Listen to a track or two whenever you want to jump-start your brain's organizational mode. Train with this song, and the effect will become more immediate and automatic.

Exercise

1. **Combine Music with Visuals.** We mentioned earlier how to combine the visual image of peaceful ocean waves and blue-green tones with smells of crisp, salty air filling your nostrils. Now try to envision this scene again with your eyes closed as you inhale that ocean breeze. Play the same sound or another selection from your playlist (e.g., "Campfire Night"), one of your favorite tranquil pieces that you know brings your thoughts into a relaxed mode. Play and replay the piece. Your goal is to connect all the sensory images into one. Try to understand your mood and state of mind, determine what direction of balance you want to achieve—more relaxed, more focused, happier—and then create a scenario in your soundscape that helps organize your intention. Play that (song, scenario, and intention) in your mind.

2. **Get Unstuck from Anything.** This exercise will help you attract solutions so that they come to you instead of you stressing out trying to hunt them down. First, find a song that has lyrics, rhythm, and vocals that take your mind into your high-energy zone. However, for this exercise, make sure the song has a message that relates to a feeling of getting unstuck, such as from a dead-end job, a relationship, a living situation, or dependency on something.

   Put the song on your iPod or MP3 player or somewhere convenient. Now think of the life situation that's got you spinning your wheels in the mud, so to speak, and feeling like you need an extra push to get out. Start by playing your song through one time. As it plays, feel its rhythm with your body. Breathe more deeply and with each inhalation, try to visualize the energy that the tune is emitting. Now put an orange lens on the energy. Maybe it looks like bright orange fog. Breathe it in. That's right—breathe the whole image in. Visualize the song's energy entering your body and mind. Visualize yourself radiating this energy. Try to empty your mind of all other thoughts.

Now play the song again and focus on the lyrics. It's easy to find any song's lyrics online. Allow the lyrics to script a movie in your mind as you listen. The scenes don't have to be literal or even have a steady progression. Just go to whatever and wherever they take you. When you come to an image that has more of an intense effect on you, see it through your orange lens and breathe it in. Remember it, and anticipate it coming around again the next time you play the song or make a whole mind-movie about just that scene. When you discover scenes you like, try to remember them, so that you can anticipate them in the future. Experiment.

Once you feel energized enough, turn off your music and view yourself in the situation that has you stuck. Don't think about it. Just see yourself in it. Let it play like a movie in your mind. Your job is to remain energized and calm. Let the solution come to you. If it doesn't come right away, don't worry. Keep your mind loose and flexible. Just stay energized. Give it time and try the whole sequence again later, maybe even the next day. Just play your song often so that you are putting its specific energy (images and all) in your memory.

Make a copy of the lyrics and read them to yourself— aloud or silently—at various times throughout the day. Many poets say they "walk" their poems to feel and finalize their rhythms. Try walking your lyrics. Feel their rhythm in your footsteps, the downbeats and pauses. Hear the song in your mind. Let your body synchronize with the words and sound. If you wind up memorizing the lyrics, you can feel their energy even more by walking them. You can even tap the song out on your office desk or elsewhere as you hear it in your mind and feel that surge of strong energy pouring through you.

Your solution will come to you, without forcing it. Don't be surprised if when you are doing nothing or something mundane, the song just pops into your head.

Chapter 7

HOW MUSIC CAN SHARPEN YOUR MEMORY

A song will outlive all sermons in the memory.

—Henry Giles

Think about what this feels like: You've lost an important piece of paperwork, and you suddenly realize that you have to recall the information it contained from memory. Or remember a time—we all have these stories—when you were typing on a computer, in the middle of composing a document—or worse, having finalized one—and right out of the blue the computer crashes. You lose your file. There is no backup. Think about that feeling.

Now imagine songwriters realizing that they have lost a whole musical score right before they are scheduled to record it. There's no shortage of this kind of story in the music world. What's interesting is that in many of them, the composer is able to quickly and accurately recall the lost, often very complex information. Science tells us that there is something we can learn from these incidents about strengthening and speeding up our own memory recall: music can give you a capacity for longer-term storage, as well as sharper and faster recall, by drawing on multiple memory banks in your brain.

One of the best stories involving a lost musical score dates back to 1973. It centers on Paul McCartney's first solo album, *Band on the Run,* and a series of events that left many mystified and catapulted the recording to iconic levels in the annals of rock and roll. The album was recorded in Laos, Nigeria—because McCartney wanted to record somewhere exotic. The trip for McCartney started out as a good idea but then took a couple of unfortunate turns. First, his entire band, with the exception of his wife, Linda, and Denny Laine, the Moody Blues guitarist, quit. Then, he and Linda found themselves stripped of their valuables at knifepoint, and their muggers ran off with all of the album's demo tapes. The demos included classics like "Band on the Run," "Bluebird," "Jet," and others. Having no backup and essentially no band left, McCartney had no choice but to rewrite all the music on the album from memory. And he did it! In the end and despite all his troubles, *Band on the Run* went on to win McCartney a Grammy Award in 1975. In fact, the album was recently remastered and rereleased around the globe, and rock critics still hail it as the best work of McCartney's solo career.

The classical world has its own share of stories like McCartney's. The nineteenth-century German composer Felix Mendelssohn found himself in a similar situation. Although Mendelssohn was not robbed at knifepoint and his score jacked, he did manage to leave in a taxi all the music he'd composed to a production of *Midsummer Night's Dream* and, like McCartney, wound up rewriting his whole piece, entirely from memory.

How is it possible for a composer to remember every note of a complicated arrangement? Is it the sequences, the beat and rhythm, the runs of notes, or is it just the way the musician hears or imagines the notes in his or her mind?

How can your brain use music as a tool to sharpen your memory, whether or not you're a musician?

How You Hold On to Information

In all cases, creating new memory involves remembering time and location, people, and events, which must be organized, categorized, and stored away. This storage is done through the process of creating new SYNAPSES, which are tiny connections on the endings of your nerve cells that store and share information. These connections help you hold on to new information.

Imbalances along the way can lead to forgetfulness, amnesia, and dementias like Alzheimer's disease. Direct damage to the brain from injury or tumor can also be a major contributor to memory problems.

With Alzheimer's, for instance, small tangles form among the nerve fibers. These tangles break up circuits and block access to the specific synapses needed to recall a particular memory or stream of knowledge, like remembering how to fix a carburetor or that the opening you see in your wall is a screen door and not a hole that has appeared overnight.

There is a direct connection between stronger memory storage and how many areas of the brain you store information in.

Interestingly, IQ, as well as the amount of information and knowledge you have amassed over your lifetime, affects the rate of mental deterioration associated with Alzheimer's. If you have a high IQ, your cognitive decline is much slower than someone with a low IQ; that's because memories are physically located throughout specialized regions of the brain. So when a tangle blocks access to one specific memory in one specific place, persons with a higher IQ tend to have multiple ways into these memories, which might be stored in a slightly different location or connected to a different area of the brain.

Imagine, for instance, someone with knowledge from both book learning and from actual hands-on experience. Typically, this person would have a wide variety of connections among a large proportion of synapses. All those connections lead to an increased level of stored knowledge on that topic. If a tangle (e.g., Alzheimer's) blocks some of the book-learning memories, she would still be able to access that same knowledge through her brain connections that store her hands-on or commonsense memories. This added capability would work for her for a while, but, in the case of Alzheimer's, as the disease progresses and more tangles form and block even more memory locations, eventually she would be left with only her oldest and most hard-wired remembrances. This is why people with severe Alzheimer's can remember only events from long ago; they lose all their more recent knowledge. But there is something we can take away from this.

Music, like the combination of book learning and hands-on experience, increases your memory storage because it increases the layers of connectivity among synapses (tapping different brain areas). And because music permeates all areas of the brain, it has a tremendous capacity to deposit any memories you attach to it in many locations. This embeds them deeper into your brain and makes it possible to retrieve them from more than one source.

This fact is important not only to people who are experiencing memory loss but also to any of us interested in optimizing our memory for daily use.

A compelling example of music's capacity to store information in multiple brain areas is evidenced in the use of music treatment for Parkinson's disease, a degenerative brain disorder characterized by muscle rigidity, tremors, and slowdown and eventual loss of body movement. It's been known for some time that exercise helps ease the symptoms and may retard the progression of the disease. However, it has recently been discovered that music, particularly in combination with dance (music and movement amplify music's effects on the brain) might be the most effective form of bringing back motor-skills memory for Parkinson's patients.

This additional and intensified storage will sharpen memory for most of us and offset imbalances for those affected by age-related forgetfulness or disease-related memory loss.

Area 22

Maybe it's hard to imagine, but we have a whole filing cabinet for everything we put into our brain, including our varied music library. When we talk about what areas of the brain perform what jobs, we use a naming structure of fifty-two distinct areas, identified by Korbinian Brodmann. AREA 22 is significant to how we can use music to improve memory. This area is located near the temporal lobe and is where you begin the process of reading musical notes and associating them with actually playing the notes or hearing them played on a musical instrument, as well as enjoying them as music. For example, you see the notes for the song "Mary Had a Little Lamb," and you can visualize yourself accurately playing the notes on an instrument or singing them or hearing them played on a piano.

This same area and its connections are also responsible for remembering everything about the way a piece of music is put together—including writing it down. At first, music is stored for the short term, such as when your brain tries to remember what was played an hour or two ago or even at the concert you attended yesterday. But say you want to deposit a song in your memory for a longer term. Then you have to replay it enough times for your brain to get the message you want the information placed in longer-term storage. Activating this brain area also helps spark the energy you need to focus—on music or anything else. So when this brain area is active, you can focus better on important information in general and on other brain areas you want to use to groove memories in accurately and deeper.

Area 19

Another area you can incorporate in your training to strengthen your long-term memory is your brain's visual processing center, which is known as AREA 19, just down the street, so to speak, from area 22. Your ability to listen, comprehend what you hear, and combine it with visuals (see it), forms a brief sketch in your brain, a quick print of the song you want to remember, and puts it deeper in your memory.

The more brain areas you use when you listen to your playlist and the more you listen, the stronger your memory storage and ability to remember information will be.

So the more elaborate and detailed your memories, the more memory storage you trigger, and the more emotion is tied to your memories, the more you will trigger those parts of the brain that control emotion and emotional storage.

The greater the variety of detail you can add to memories (e.g., emotional, motor, sound, visual, language, color, scent, touch), the easier it is for all of it to stream into the memory and into more parts of the brain.

And that's exactly what we are going for.

Using Your Playlist to Enhance Memory

Here is an example of how you can use your playlist to enhance your memory: Imagine a young woman who has been working for a business consulting firm for a few years. The firm recently signed a deal with a professional education outfit to film a series of half-hour educational podcasts involving techniques that business managers can use to

improve employee job satisfaction and on-the-job performance. The podcasts will be sold online for $0.99 each and
will be widely available. Her employer has asked her to do
one of the podcasts because it is good publicity for the firm
and because she is articulate, friendly, and telegenic. She
enjoys giving presentations, but she has always used either a
flip chart or PowerPoint. She is scheduled to film the pod-
cast soon. She wants to look poised and natural, and so she
would like to deliver most of the presentation without having
to read a script.

She has decided to use music to enhance her memory of
the script. She feels that her energy and mind-set are a little
off—she's too jumpy—to get started, so she plays her favorite
relaxing track, titled "Campfire Night," which she found at
the iTunes Store. The soundtrack works especially well for her
because she lives in a rural area where you can have open fires
on your property, and she and her family have enjoyed many
nights camping on their own land with peaceful campfires
and lots of stargazing. She has many positive feelings attached
to these sounds, and now they come in handy, helping her
mellow out. She closes her eyes and brings to mind one of her
favorite nights sitting around the campfire with her family and
watching a meteor shower. She tries to remember the finer
details of the night. She plays her relaxing track for about
five to seven minutes. This takes any edge off and balances
her. It also—importantly—gets her brain in the right mode
for remembering.

Once she feels more balanced and full of positive
emotions, she puts on an activating song from her "Best

Memories" playlist. She chooses "Stayin' Alive" from *Saturday Night Fever*. She loves to dance, and *Saturday Night Fever* is one of her all-time favorite movies. She has fond memories of how she and her college roommates used to watch old dance movies in the dorms and how they would go out dancing until all hours of the night. She remembers "Stayin' Alive" by the Bee Gees was always a big hit on the dance floors. She has used this song many times to get her head in the right place to begin to commit things to memory. It makes her feel alert and puts her into a remembering mood with her mind flowing.

By playing this tune right after "Campfire Night," she is able to ramp up these effects. She plays the tune a few times and walks around her office (throwing in a few dance moves) as she listens and remembers. This keeps her energy high and her mind focused. She finds that playing the tune when she reads any text interferes, so instead she turns off the music and reads her presentation aloud—walking around her office as she does. Her walking around and vocalizing deepens her memory of the script as well. Her brain is energized, focused, and in the right mood to remember. She is at her best. She reads the script a few more times without music. The repetition sends her brain the message that she wants to remember this information. She practices this regimen on and off up until the day of her preparation. Her routine helps make long-term memorization of her pitch successful.

The Bee Gees classic works for her, but for you, it could be any song you like. In the end, it is your choice. What's important is the following:

- Get in balance first.
- Pick a feel-good song with fast, upbeat rhythm and good memories from your more distant past.
- Get your brain into its remembering mode by playing your song several times and bringing back (in fine detail) all the good memories that it generates.
- Practice reading and memorizing your text without music.
- Use this regimen to continue practicing.

As you continue to practice, your brain will get the message faster and start putting itself into a remembering mode more quickly and easily.

The following is a sample memory playlist from an individual who is familiar with our techniques. You will notice that it uses dance tunes.

Sample "Memory" Playlist

▸ **"Love Shack,"** The B-52s

▸ **"Everybody Dance Now,"** C+C Music Factory

▸ **"Good Vibrations,"** Marky Mark and the Funky Bunch

▸ **"Unbelievable,"** EMF

▸ **"The Power,"** Snap!

The Emotional Factor

To use music to improve memory, you want to amp up its capacity to store specific information in multiple areas of the brain. We have previously talked about the strong connections between music and your emotions and between music and your fight-or-flight responses. In general, the more emotional or traumatic an event, the stronger your recollection of that event will be. Emotional memory recall is so strong that you can feel, in a millisecond, that you are right back in a scene from your past—even from years ago—reliving it all over again. The release of adrenaline during such events and in remembering them grooves them deeper into your memory.

The reason for all of this is that when you store highly emotional information, you are tapping into an essential drive that nature has installed in your brain to help you survive. It can launch you straight to your most powerful and quickest mental and physical settings. This is why many people can hear just a few bars of their high school or college alma mater song and be right back there. Or hear a song like Jimi Hendrix's "Purple Haze" or "Hey Joe" or Jefferson Airplane's "White Rabbit" or Iron Butterfly's "In-A-Gadda-Da-Vida" and instantly zap into the sights, smells, events, and people that were in their world when those tunes came out in the 1960s or where they were when they discovered them. Or it might be the 1990s with the Cranberries' "Zombie," REM's "Losing My Religion," Rage Against the Machine's "Killing in the Name," or Green Day's "Time of Your Life." Listen to the whole song and you can remember incredibly specific detail: someone who sat next to you in homeroom when you were in junior high school, the color of that person's shirt, a scent like deodorant, a specific televised news report, a specific subject or a specific incident, and so on.

Sound has had this triggering effect on memory through-out human evolution. This is because it gives us quick recall of information when we need it. Looking back through the zoom lens of time, a person's sensitivity to sound could have meant life or death—as we mentioned earlier, when our ancestors saw a lion coming at him, it was probably too late to escape. But if he could hear its approach, he might have a running chance.

Although we won't see many lions coming at us today, we still rely on that same sort of auditory capability in an infinite variety of scenarios. Anyone, for example, who has ever had to speak to a roomful of people knows this lesson of sound—partners know it; parents know it too. You can tell where another family member is in the house, for example, just by the sounds he or she is making. You can tell when someone you know is angry by the sound you hear when he or she turns the pages of a newspaper or sets something down on the table. These sounds and what they mean are all in your memory.

Public speakers may read from a text, but their ears are perked to sounds that tell them how things are going. Sounds like "uh-huh," "yes," or the beginning of an applause signal that things are going well. In contrast, sounds like the rustling of paperwork or other items, doors opening and closing, or mutterings of disagreement indicate that things may not be working out so well. Sounds can in many cases signal more information than pages of words—and fast. How many words would it take to convey all the meaning behind a cat's purr or hiss or a person's "mmm"? Or a deep breath someone you know takes when agitated but still one step away from taking a stance against what you're saying? Our memories of these sounds help us know what's coming next and begin to navigate things to our advantage.

Music in Action

Ancient ceremonies in many cultures of the world (like South Africa and Peru) provide another good example of how musical memory works. Most of these ceremonies include an abundance of chants and songs, and they use a lot of repetition. The ancients intuitively knew, as primitive people knew everywhere on the globe, that if they could put important ideas in a combined package of music, words, images, and emotion—and if people repeated it enough times—it would have staying power in their minds. No matter what your religious beliefs, this is fascinating culturally, and scientifically it helps you see how music (particularly once associated with different brain areas) has historically been treated as a tool to help you train your mind to remember things.

Take, as another example, the song "Twinkle, Twinkle, Little Star," which many of us hummed along to at a very early age, then later learned the lyrics to, and then after that were able to sing in chorus with others. Do you remember it? Can you sing it right now? How about "Jingle Bells" or some other holiday songs you listened to every year as a child? Your memory will spark whether you actively sang along or just passively listened to these tunes—or any other tunes for that matter.

Many politicians use a chant-like structure in their speeches. We've all heard this technique because it is so popular and gets us to remember things like campaign slogans. For example, we all remember President Obama's "Yes We Can," chant which he used in his speech for the New Hampshire primary and then again in his acceptance speech as president-elect:

> Yes we can to justice and equality.
> Yes we can to opportunity and prosperity.
> Yes we can heal this nation.
> Yes we can repair this world.
> Yes we can.

All you have to do is hear a brief sample, and you can experience how the speech has been stored in various parts of your brain: you can hear it, feel it, and perhaps even see it.

Professional musicians memorizing songs for performance are also a great example of how repetition and music makes perfect. In fact, every aspect of memory and music we have discussed so far is what enabled McCartney and Mendelssohn both to dip into their memory tanks and successfully remember their lost music.

▸▸ I remember when I started learning how to play Irish dance tunes on my blue electric violin. I love those songs. They are fast and fun to play, and hardly anyone can stay in their seat when they hear one. You have to dance.

Anyway, there were a lot of notes to some of the tunes, so I would learn them a few notes at a time, off a sheet of music, and play my section *du jour* several times in between other songs. The repetition helped me commit them to memory—and not just the notes either, but the way I rocked the bow and any nuances I'd throw in that weren't in the music itself, like when I'd speed things up toward the end and just how fast I would take it or any special electronic effects I'd toss in. I enjoyed practicing my violin at the end of a long day, and in no time, I would have a new dance piece committed to memory and could play it out without any sheet music. Sometimes I only played the tunes once a year—for St. Patrick's Day—but I'd remember them. Even now, I can remember them without much effort—and not just the notes but all the little extras too.
—Joseph

Choreographers and dancers offer another good example of how to use music and repetition. Both use musical accompaniment to aid in learning and memorizing a performance. After doing the same sequences many times, you can do them smoothly, with confidence, and virtually automatically.

The more you enjoy a musical piece, the more you will remember it.

Here's why. To comprehend and process any information, including musical information, the temporal lobes have to first absorb and take in all the events that are occurring, which have to be sorted through and picked clean of any important information, like the homework you just finished or the look of the most beautiful man or woman you've ever seen.

All the while, the unimportant details of the day—like all the cars you passed on the way to work or what exactly you read as you looked at the newspaper headlines on the train—all disappear by the time you awake the next day from a restful sleep. The key is keeping important information alive, typically by giving it emotional content, which increases with any personal meaning that you attach to the information. For example, a particular song feels good and was also the song you used to play in your Jeep, with the top down, and your best friend riding shotgun on most Saturday nights when you were eighteen; or another one was the perfect song to listen to on your drive to the beach this summer.

It helps to find more ways to like your favorite songs, especially by developing new habits for listening more closely, as we mentioned in chapter 2. For example, you can find places in the lyrics that may have current emotional meaning for you. Listen to your song over and over until you have memorized every detail of it. This repetition will push your brain to deepen your memory of the song by streaming every aspect of it within the cluster of circuits that store all the related details of your thoughts and feelings as you appreciate your tune. You can modify the memory with any emotional updates you wish to add, such as visualizing your spouse or partner and you in your Jeep on a great sunny day, wind blowing in your hair, just flowing together, free and happy, without a care in the world except each other.

The more you listen to the same fragments of music, the more your brain tries to remember them and relate them to other events in your life.

Just as the employee trying to memorize her pitch for the company used a dance tune and her college memories to launch her brain into memory mode, you can do the same. All you have to do is start associating some of your strongest positive memories with your favorite song, and then you can use them to help you remember other things. To do this:

- Preferably find songs from a time in your past that already have positive, strong memory associations and put them on your playlist.
- Make new song memories. It's possible for you to attach any information you wish to musical fragments and to remember them for the long term. Again, the hallmark of this skill is connecting three sources of information in your brain: visual, musical, and lyrical. You do this by taking a piece of music, connecting it to an emotional image, and making a story out of it in your mind (language). The whole narrative plays like a mind-movie, a short film (visual), in your head. Because you associate four specific components (musical, emotional, visual, and lyrical), your brain streams the memory deeper and wider, making it sharper and quicker to recall.

Anyone can learn to improve memory by using music. Let's say, for example, your wife were about to deliver her first baby tomorrow, and today you are sending the song "Child of Mine" by Carole King to all your contacts and friends to share your joy and happiness in the upcoming news.

That song's connections to your life are already incredibly

strong and capable of forming an association in your brain to put it in your musical file cabinet for long-term storage. But what if the song has some additional emotional meaning for you, say, a romantic memory? That connection would amplify its meaning and help you store the file even longer, maybe for a lifetime, also making it readily available for rapid recall. Whenever you hear the song afterward, you won't be able just to hear it anymore. Your mind and emotional memory will bring into your consciousness the series of associations to which the musical fragment has already been connected.

Don't forget about fragrance. What if, for example, a particular fragrance is connected to a specific piece of music that you remember very well because the association was made, for example, when you met your husband? The music and lyrics and the fragrance of your husband's cologne, along with all the details of that first meeting, are etched into your memory. And they all come rushing back at once by just hearing that song again or when your husband is wearing that cologne.

But why wait until you need help to put your brain in remembering mode? We suggest that you start today. Have fun. Use songs that either already have strong emotional connections for you or find new songs.

To make new memories, play songs when you are on vacation or when you and your partner are romantic. When you read a scene or chapter from your favorite book or poem, play a song and make a memory of that. Make music part of your adventures: hiking, camping, picnics, sight-seeing. Then put your new memories on your playlist and carry them in your pocket.

Sample "Best Memories" Playlist No. 1

▶ **"Love Shack,"** The B52s

▶ **"Everybody Dance Now,"** C+C Music Factory

▶ **"Good Vibrations,"** Marky Mark and the Funky Bunch

▶ **"Unbelievable,"** EMF

▶ **"The Power,"** Snap!

Sample "Best Memories" Playlist No. 2

▶ **"Wind Song,"** Wandering Endorphin

▶ **"Rocky Mountain High,"** John Denver

▶ **"Heaven,"** Bryan Adams

▶ **"I Want to Know What Love Is,"** Foreigner

▶ **"(Looking for) The Heart of Saturday Night,"** Tom Waits

Putting Together Your Playlist

Here is how to begin choosing songs for a playlist that will help sharpen your memory.

- **First, pick songs you like a lot.**
- **Pay attention to when a certain song works and when it doesn't.**
- **Ingrain songs into your memory.**
- **Make a playlist that is task oriented. Train your brain with your assembled playlist.**
- **Look for new and old songs.**
- **Use guided imagery.**
- **Use a song's BPM to help you organize your playlist.**
- **Use your emotional connections to songs.**
- **Use your brain's reward system.**
- **Use songs you can empathize with.**
- **Use songs with useful metaphors.**
- **Use songs with strong and obvious rhythms.**
- **Attach your best memories to songs**. Start attaching your best memories to songs you are already connected to emotionally. We also encourage you to discover new tunes. Use upbeat songs with faster rhythms. Create a story in your head that you can associate with your song. Use plenty of visual detail in your story. Put together a playlist of these songs. Use them to get your brain in remembering mode.

Exercise

1. **Your Five- to Ten-Minute Busy-Day Fix.** Say you have at most five to ten minutes here and there during the day. It's OK! Even very busy people have a favorite warm and soothing song, maybe a lullaby or something you like to calm down with. Put on your favorite soothing song. Now sit yourself in a comfortable chair (it's just five minutes, come on!), close your eyes, and create the image of ocean waves or a beautiful garden. Incorporate fragrance—maybe from a small bottle of your favorite essential oil that you might keep at your desk. Next time you have a meeting or presentation and have the luxury of a few moments of prep time, open that soothing narrative up in your mind and play it through. Then think about what you need to do at your meeting. This will tune your thoughts to your associative memory, which will help you relax and sharpen your ability to recall the information you need. And practice, practice, practice to make things perfect!

2. **Train Your Associative Memory.** Find a quiet place and relax. You likely already have a meditative piece of music that you like to listen to that helps you get into a meditative mood. Your musical choice could be soothing sounds of ocean waves, rain falling on trees, or something that strikes you from India, Tibet, Mexico, or Peru and brings you quickly into that state of mind.

   Slow your breathing down and try to breathe more deeply, breathing in through your nose and out through your mouth. Count as you breathe in: one, two, three, four. Then pause, hold your breath for a similar length of time, and then gently breathe out through your mouth, to a count of four. This is called measured breathing and helps get you into a nice relaxed and focused state. Keep breathing slowly this way, and let your whole body loosen up and start feeling comfort in slowing down. Now visualize a current situation that brings joy and warmth into your life. Let your mind look around in this situation as you visualize it. See yourself in the situation, as though it were a movie, not becoming anxious, staying cool, and going with the flow of everything that presents itself. Let each feel-good thought and picture that comes to you float across your mind like a reflection on water. Consider a wider range of actions you could employ in the situation that would nurture more good and joy for everyone involved. Visualize yourself flowing into these actions.

Now, add in the sense of smell, say, lavender oil or some other fragrance you love. This will further immerse you in that particular meditative state. Then, with practice, the next time you perform these steps and associations using the combination of meditation, visualization, story, sound, and fragrance, your brain can more rapidly form that associative set of memories and guide you into your meditative bliss. Do this often, and when the situation you have visualized presents itself in your daily life, you will have trained your brain to use its memory to absorb even more joy from it.

3. **Use Associative Memory to Achieve Goals.** Follow the meditation prescribed in Exercise 2. Instead of visualizing a

current situation that brings joy and warmth into your life, visualize a goal that you would like to achieve. This can be anything from getting a promotion at work to improving an interpersonal relationship to an athletic accomplishment. Consider a wide range of specific behaviors and actions that you could employ to facilitate your achievement of this goal. See yourself doing these things, as well as people's responses to them. Visualize yourself flowing into your selected actions, again as if you were in a movie. See yourself as the lead character, not becoming anxious, staying cool, and going with the flow of everything that presents itself—achieving the most good for you and for everyone else too. Practice this meditation often, and when the situation you have visualized (and committed to memory) presents itself in real life, you will have trained your brain to act accordingly.

Chapter 8

HOW TO USE MUSIC TO IMPROVE YOUR MOOD

Music is the shorthand of emotion.

—Leo Tolstoy

usic can shift your mood instantly. Most of us have been stuck at a red light when the car next to us is blasting music so loud that it feels like a space shuttle is about to launch right next to you. If what's playing is something torturous to your musical ear, you can't wait for the light to change so you can escape. But there are times, however, when sound blasting from some unexpected source ignites positive and pleasurable feelings, and you wouldn't mind hearing the whole tune.

Your playlist can have this same kind of instant mood-altering capability, giving you control over your feelings when you want it, at a moment's notice.

You can use your favorite songs to get you in a mood or out of a mood, to improve your mood, and to sustain a mood. This all must start, however, with developing an awareness of how individual tunes influence your feelings and what you think about and how you tend to behave when you hear them. There is a certain amount of common sense involved. For example, you tend to play something upbeat if you are feeling down. Or you might play something slow if you are anxious. These are good places to start in getting a little more sensitive to the effects of music.

You might know that already, but this book is all about kicking it up a notch, which you can learn to do quite easily. One thing you can do is try to pay attention to what you need to be hearing in a given situation and to think about what you absolutely don't need to hear.

For example, let's say that you have a great playlist for getting you to work happy on any average day. You call it "Morning Drive," and you are totally satisfied with it, even if you are always open to adding a new song that makes you feel terrific. For the most part, you aren't going to mess much with a playlist that works. Now let's consider a not-so-average morning.

Say that you've gotten up and are feeling a little slow this morning. You are heading out the door when your partner, who is irritated over something, opens up a discussion over an issue that is bothering him or her. The next thing you know, things get pretty touchy because you have a difference of opinion. Hard as you try to keep things from getting more agitated, they do. You resolve your differences enough to leave in peace, yet you are still feeling the effects of having begun your day with conflict.

You get in your car and think to put on your "Morning Drive" playlist. But then you decide not to. You make this decision because the last time you were in a similar situation, you did put it on, and that mistake almost took away the play-list's power. Not only didn't the playlist shift you out of your down beat, agitated mood, but you also began to associate the music with the negative incident rather than with all of the good stuff it was already attached to. You turned off the playlist before any negative associations took root, because you know that the playlist works because you have associated each song with positive feelings, memories, and images. So you definitely don't want to change that association.

If you can't use your "Morning Drive" playlist, what should you use? You remember a song you and your partner used to listen to by 10,000 Maniacs. Your partner had the song on one of the CDs you used to listen to together when you first met. In fact, your partner turned you on to the group. You associated the CD with your partner right away, realizing that he or she played it everywhere. Soon it became one of your favorites too. Your favorite song on the CD is "These Are the Days." So you find it on your iPod and hit "play."

You start to hear the beautiful uplifting melody and rhythms and then Natalie Merchant sings the lines you have always loved so much: "You are blessed by something / That will grow and bloom in you." That's all you need, and you are in a better place already. Your emotions, your imagery, the words, the story you are now seeing unfold in your mind and that is being rewarded by your brain (remember the influence of dopamine) are all coordinated and working to make you feel better and see the bigger picture. You feel your agitation dissolve and your thoughts focus on the depth of agreement you and your partner have on important things. This agreement is at the core of your relationship with your partner. Your positive feelings grow as you hear the song, so you play it several times. It puts you where you need to be for your daily tasks and where you want to be when you return home.

This is just one example of how you can use your playlist to significantly decrease (or short-circuit) one way of feeling and replace it with a completely different way of feeling. As another example, perhaps you're doing some mundane work—painting a room, filing papers, stacking wood—and you feel kind of blah. Playing some mildly arousing music can help you direct your thoughts away from the uninteresting, deenergizing experience so that you can put your mind in a state of flow as you work. Then, rather than walk away from the work sapped and unfocused, you can walk away with an energized and flowing mind-set that you can transfer to other goals.

▸▸ For several years I've been listening to the British group Muse. I find them to be amazingly gifted in playing, with many different qualities in their sound that influence my brain. They can move my emotions from high to low, just in how they modulate the tones and frequencies of their instruments. When I started listening to them, they sounded like many other artists I had heard before (e.g., King Crimson, Queen, Kruder & Dorfmeister, and Guns N' Roses). Nonetheless, their fantastic use of mixture in the combination and modulation of their instruments makes them universally superior, for me, to these other groups.

Lyrically, they are very psychologically minded. Their

titles are pretty emotionally connected—such as "Uprising," "Undisclosed Desires," "Resistance," "Feeling Good," and "Unintended." The depth of their lyrics combined with the intensity of their instrumentals can instantly create a desired state of mind for me.

—Galina

As for playlist suggestions, the type of tune you pick from your playlist to get you out of a mildly low mood depends on your preferences and experiences. Classical music can help you shift your feelings just as well as modern alternative rock, as might the constantly changing rhythm and beat of hip-hop. Tunes like "Every Breath You Take" by the Police or the Beatles' "Here Comes the Sun" chime a worry-free tone and are generally good for putting you in a take-it-easy spirit.

Other times, however, you might need to blast open your eyes to get out of an emotional funk. These are times when you need to instantly up your flow of adrenaline. In these cases, you might want to select more aggressive songs like "Caught in a Mosh" by Anthrax, "Mechanix" by Megadeth, or Alice in Chains' "Whatcha Gonna Do." Some people might like being blasted out of their lows by a melody like Queen's "The Show Must Go On," which has power in both its musical and its lyrical qualities. The point is that you have lots of choice.

The following is a sample playlist intended to get the listener out of mild lows and into a higher, more flowing mood.

Sample "Out of the Blahs" Playlist

▸ **"Angel of the Morning,"** The Pretenders

▸ **"Because the Night,"** 10,000 Maniacs

▸ **"Like a Rolling Stone,"** Bob Dylan

▸ **"Touch of Grey,"** Grateful Dead

▸ **"Love the One You're With,"** Crosby, Stills, and Nash

The following is a sample playlist intended to blast the listener out of mild lows and into a higher, more flowing mood.

Sample "Blasting Out the Blahs" Playlist

▸ **"Baba O'Riley,"** The Who

▸ **"Numb,"** Linkin Park

▸ **"No Way Back,"** Foo Fighters

▸ **"You're Going Down,"** Sick Puppies

▸ **"Fight Fire with Fire,"** Metallica

Let's examine another instance when you might use your playlist to get out of one mood and into another. Say you are jumpy. You know, from past experience, that when you feel this way, it is easy for you to overreact, often in important situations. Why not try using music's connection with your emotional network to swing your mind and body into a more favorable state by listening to some blues or another style of music that has the same effect on you. Yes, this may sadden you a bit and bring you down. But it can quickly reset your psychic and physical energy so you're not so jumpy, back into the state of balance at which you can perform at your optimum. You just have to remember to be moderate in how you use this kind of tune.

Let's get into some specifics. You're jumpy and headed to an important meeting. You may find that listening beforehand to something bluesy, like ZZ Top's "Blue Jean Blues" or Sarah McLachlan's "Angel," fits the bill because those songs might slow your thoughts (and reaction point) down to a level that will sharpen your empathy and enable you to more accurately identify people's feelings, read their expressions, listen better, speak in turn, and most important, keep from overreacting. A little melancholy, for you, is just what's needed in this situation—but only when you really need it on those days when your edgy feelings may be overwhelming you. And only just enough—you don't want to make yourself too laidback.

Sometimes you're jumpy in a different way. Say you are trying to wind down at home after a hard day at work, and all you want to hear is silence. You are not ready for a conversation, you're not ready to make dinner, and you just need some peace and quiet, just for a few minutes. In this case, something like white noise can do the trick, something you don't have to think about, something soothing and mindless. There are several varieties of white noise. The most common is the hissing sound you hear when all other sound has been washed out of all audible frequencies. Natural versions of white noise are surf sounds or rain falling on trees or crickets, nighttime pond sounds, and the like. The point is that it's nothing you have to think about to enjoy. At times like this, just the solitude of not thinking can really improve your mood. Try downloading some white noise for occasions like this one.

Improving Your Mood—Together

You can also use your playlist to influence your mood and your partner's mood together. As you have seen, you can build a playlist from almost any experience. Try creating one based on your shared memories of an event or trip you have taken together, maybe that time in New York City, Boulder, the Caribbean, or Mexico that you both loved because you were so worry-free. Why not pull out that recording of Bob Marley or Jimmy Buffett that played a lot on that cruise you took together? Do you think this might be too corny? It might be, but it also might work. Psychologically speaking, sharing music can actually give you both that moment of united musical emotionality that you previously enjoyed so much in the earlier days of your relationship.

What if you are both angry and tired, and you feel that you just can't say anything nice to each other? Again, try to find a piece of music that you both love—maybe some songs from your wedding day. When one man's wife started picking on him because she was irritable after a long day at work, he used the Temptations' "You Are My Everything," a song they played at their wedding. He started playing the song at a very low volume, barely audible, and he would increase the volume slowly until she heard the song playing and saw him with a smile on his face; then she started laughing, and her anger was gone.

Music Can Help Relieve the Pain

Music can be used as a means of catharsis, which is the process of bringing to the surface repressed negative emotions, complexes, and feelings in an effort to identify and relieve yourself of them. We all have been through some form of emotional catharsis triggered in us by music—at weddings and funerals, anniversaries and birthdays, events that music and song almost always accompany.

Eric Clapton's song "Tears in Heaven" provides a moving example of a cathartic experience. Clapton wrote the song about the death of his four-year-old son Conor, who fell to his death out of an apartment window in 1991. Clapton did an interview with the Australian Nine Network's show *60 Minutes*, in which the interviewer expressly asked Clapton about his son's tragic death. "Was writing about Conor your way of dealing with the tragedy and great loss?"

▸▸ Sometimes music doesn't match the mood. I recently attended a formal dinner with a group of individuals who had participated in a presentation I had given at a university. The ambiance in the room was warm and inviting. The restaurant, however, decided to blare its musical selections into the dining room. The loud music interfered with the warm celebratory conversation we were going for. It intruded on our mood and when the management was unable to lower the volume beyond a certain point, it brought a quick sense of anxiety into the room, which quickly spread. Once the first complaint surfaced, other people chimed in with complaints, and this spread into other areas besides the loud music. I took notice of the downward dive the once ambient atmosphere was now taking and had to ward off my own urges to follow.

—Joseph

"Yeah. Writing and playing," Clapton said. "Playing…well first and foremost, the most healing experience was for me just to hold my guitar and play and make music. Make music that made…that took me away."

All anyone has to do is listen to the song and to know how Clapton felt at the moment. "Yeah. My question was, Will I see you again?" explained Clapton. "It was very simple. I mean, in a sense it wasn't even a sad song, it was a song of belief…where it talks about there will be no more tears in heaven, you know. And I think it was…a song of optimism."

Clapton's sadness is cleansing—for him and for us. He mentioned receiving at least 150 letters a day from people saying that they knew his grief. As the interviewer comments, in that dark hour, Clapton became the "universal artist," perhaps providing people with a place to park their grief for a moment, experience their own catharsis, and carry them with him to a better, more optimistic place.

Using Music as an Interlude

Say your goal is to just have a good night out with your friends after a stressful week at work. Try to find some songs that will get you ready for a night out on the town with your friends. When you listen, try to amp up the feel-good effect, visualizing the performers playing live or imagining yourself already out having fun, maybe with a certain someone you like or away from the kids and alone with your thoughts for ten minutes without having to feel self-conscious about it. What matters is that your music helps you think about positive events as you get yourself ready and plan for the events of the evening.

Using music to link actions and goals (in this case, a desired mood) can require some significant practice in using your playlist. Even if a song works for you, it might not work the same if you're in different moods. One patient learned that listening to a favorite piece of music when he was already feeling good really pumped him up even higher. But when he was angry, it was the worst thing for him to hear. It was filled with high-frequency music, loud, bawdy language that he liked, but when he was already in a bad mood, it only made him feel angrier.

He discovered that when he was angry, his brain was more agreeable with pop songs like Justin Bieber's "My World" or even Taylor Swift's "Speak Now," a song he heard at a lounge while engaged in a conversation, sipping iced tea, and feeling very calm. Now he carries these two pieces of music on his iPod in case he needs to "treat" his anger when he gets provoked. He reports experiencing significantly fewer angry outbursts and having better control of them when they get sparked.

Many individuals say that, although they don't know how, after using music in this way, they care less about what got them into their mood in the first place and are able to get on with things peacefully once again. Can you imagine how much more peaceful our universe could become if people could learn to listen to more music, instead of fighting and yelling at each other, and worse? All our relationships could become like a symphony!

Use Music to Predict Emotions

You can use music to identify and clarify how you are feeling at a specific moment of time or even where you are headed in the near future. This comes in handy because it can help keep potential negative emotions from intruding on your flow and let you use the raw power of positive emotions to fuel your best mind-set.

Certain songs help you see into your emotional profile and predict where you will be—emotionally—in a few minutes or further down the line. This capability can help you identify a problematic mood before it happens and before it causes you a problem. Or it can identify an emotion to enhance so that you have its energy when you need it. Music can do this because it is linked to your self-awareness. Here is how this works.

Say you strongly identify with a song. You can use that feeling to better understand yourself. Imagine that you are heading to a job interview, for example, and you feel compelled to play Ozzy Osbourne's "Crazy Train" or Guns N' Roses' "Welcome to the Jungle," possibly because you are not happy about the interview. You lost a job and you're interviewing for a new, less preferable job. Here's a great opportunity to use the songs as an emotional "scan."

Ask yourself, "What is being said in the song? How does this pertain to me? How can I use the feelings it evokes to my advantage? Can I use them to help bolster my self-confidence?" Then use the high energy of the music to refocus on where you are headed, and visualize yourself there, acting in confidence, in control, and flowing. What mood do you need to be in? What memories can be activated that will facilitate your positive thoughts and emotions? Where is your state of balance, and do you need to adjust one way or the other to feel you are in the best place you can be?

So maybe the high-powered energy of the guitar in "Crazy Train" makes you feel a sense of catharsis as Ozzy sings, "Life's a bitter shame" and that your wounds "aren't healing." Or like Axl Rose sings, "You know where you are / You're in the jungle baby." So maybe you agree. It's a jungle out there. You feel more catharsis. But the high energy of the music brings out the defiance in you and makes you want to put up the good fight. Axl Rose screams, "If you've got a hunger for what you see/ you'll take it eventually." Psychologically, your mood of defiance can call forth other similar thoughts and memories to increase it.

This wouldn't be a good idea if your own wounds sweep you away into a zone that isn't best for your interview. And this is a predictable direction you could take. However, you can choose to grab on to all the energy in the songs and use it to rocket you into a strong and confident and awake demeanor, defying your ill luck in losing your previous job and boosting your confidence to acquire and take on this new one.

By doing this, you have enhanced your options to choose what happens next to you—to take some control over the situation. This kind of thinking can take you off a potentially destructive track and put you on a more organized and constructive one that moves you forward in sync with where you need to be at the moment to simultaneously contribute to and get the most from your life.

Music to Heal a Broken Heart

Sometimes our choice is not to listen to a particular type of music that projects the wrong emotions. Often when a person is involved in a breakup, he or she might say, "I can't stand listening anymore to lyrics that are even remotely connected to love." One such individual recently commented, "I was driving today and heard 'You Are My Love' by Jim Reeves on the radio. I started crying uncontrollably and had to pull the car off the road." Interestingly, however, that same person later admitted to hearing the same song again, in three months' time, and being able to appreciate its deep and beautiful effects again—without any of the formerly painful emotional pull.

This is a very good example of how you need to restrict

yourself from certain music sometimes—as when you are in a vulnerable state of mind, such as a breakup.

Instead, you want to be gentle to yourself by not taking, or even think of taking, your mind to these love-land songs. What really helps during these tender times are funny children's songs. Get yourself a CD with funny music and lyrics, especially when the content is about different animals and their sounds, and practice singing along with them!

One individual was feeling bad enough after a breakup to call in sick to work, and he stayed home for a week. He found that listening to any kind of music that remotely reminded him of romance made him feel worse. So he started listening to Green Day's cover of "Teenage Lobotomy," a song he used to listen to with his buddies in college before their soccer games. This worked to get him in a good mood before the games. He found that every time he played the song now, he would stop thinking (or obsessing) about his relationship. He put the song on his iPod and started playing it several times a day. By the end of the week, he felt good enough to return to work. For the next month, whenever he had unbearable thoughts of the breakup, he'd play his song, and that helped him through this acute phase of his broken heart.

Music to Pull You Out of a Mood

It is also possible to use music that influences your brain's emotional network to pull you out of a dysfunctional mood. For example, say people tell you that you are always late for things. Let's see, how about we start from the morning. Is it hard to wake up? Hard to manage your time before leaving for work? Perhaps it is difficult to leave the house because you are just not feeling with it enough to get your act together. You feel a little down and find yourself pacing back and forth thinking about this or that, one more thing that you need to say to your partner or kids.

When you are able to identify what holds you back, you may want to change it. And of course, if you want to make a change, music will be your friend.

In the aforementioned situation, music can help you to speed up your own brain-wave frequencies, in the morning and bring you to work on time. No magic, just a little training. One individual in a reportedly similar circumstance used music from his childhood. He changed his wake-up music so that he was greeted with tunes from his childhood summer camp, a place where everybody had to rise and shine and literally get themselves in a straight line and ready to go, go, go. That memory of childhood discipline, spunk, and timing translated into strong playlist medicine that has helped him manage a speedy and organized departure from his house—which used to take him a few hours before.

One particular patient who cut herself to soothe or calm down learned that listening to the same relaxing music on repeat while moving rhythmically with the sounds was very helpful in reducing her anxiety. This helped her transit out from a charged emotionally reactive state and into a calmer thinking and more controlled mind-set.

You also can use your playlist to eliminate self-destructive thoughts, feelings, and tendencies by replacing them with a more positive mind-set. Let's say you're feeling too anxious and overwhelmed, and you want to minimize your panic. Operating in this mind-set makes it difficult to find a solution. Maybe you are feeling pressured at work to complete a project and time is running out. Or maybe you are trying to juggle two jobs, take care of your family, and take night classes at your area college. The point is that you feel overwhelmed. This triggers self-destructive thoughts and feelings. Your panic can make you feel like giving up or self-medicating (e.g., with drugs or alcohol) to feel better. If so, as for the patient described earlier, you want to select some purely relaxing brain music, maybe something that's just instrumental, raindrops falling on leaves, ocean waves, slow jazz or soft, slow classical music—music to calm, relax, and comfort you. Don't use anything that will add more anxiety to your mind.

Use your calming music to help you rebalance the fast and slow frequencies that occur when your thoughts move into a panic state. When you experiment and find out what music works best, then you can save those songs on your iPod or MP3 player, knowing that any one of the scores can help rebalance your feelings. You can use your most effective playlist track to then smoothly sway your mind away from destructive tendencies and back toward a healthier mind-set. Then you can reevaluate what has triggered you and decide on your best solution.

Maybe you feel empty and want to resort to harmful and self-destructive behaviors to get that rush of excitement and pleasure. Self-destructive behaviors can promote the release of endorphins—neurochemical substances in your body that excite you and make you feel like you're high and that life is good. An individual feeling this way may be lacking certain neurotransmitters or have an abundance of one kind or another that is causing an imbalance. Often medications are prescribed in such situations.

But it is possible to pull yourself out of these feelings and accompanying behaviors by activating some of your body's top-shelf neurochemicals. You can do this by using your playlist to increase your brain rhythms and by playing some stimulating, very fast songs, the type you hear in dance clubs. Have you seen how some people look like they are high on the music, swaying and bobbing to the beat with their eyes fixed, almost in a trance? You can learn to use music intentionally to achieve this heightened state of mental arousal without the need for extra recreational substances or self-destructive behaviors. Activating your brain's emotional systems might be the best way for you to redirect negative thoughts and prevent self-destructive behaviors from occurring. Of course, in all of these instances, balance is the key!

Identify what you want to change and look through your musical library to find songs that have produced the desired effect on you before. Try to match them up with your current goal of improving your personality and who it is you want to be.

Putting Together Your Playlist

Here is how to begin choosing songs for a playlist that will help you improve your mood.

- **First, pick songs you like a lot.**
- **Pay attention to when a certain song works and when it doesn't.**
- **Ingrain songs into your memory.**
- **Make a playlist that is task oriented. Train your brain with your assembled playlist.**
- **Look for new and old songs.**
- **Use guided imagery.**
- **Use a song's BPM to help you organize your playlist.**
- **Use your emotional connections to songs.**
- **Use your brain's reward system.**
- **Use songs you can empathize with.**
- **Use songs with useful metaphors.**
- **Use songs with strong and obvious rhythms.**
- **Attach your best memories to songs.**
- **Eliminate destructive thoughts and actions.** Start putting together a playlist of songs that you have found that can intervene when you are in a mood that spawns destructive thoughts or actions. Use calming, relaxing music. Once you put together a playlist, use it to train your brain out of these patterns when they occur.

Exercise

1. **Enjoy Your Drive to Work.** What's best for you while you are driving to work and irritable? It's good to have a pick of soothing melodies on your playlist. The most important thing is that you try to shift your mood to a better mind-set by using a tune or tunes to which you are emotionally connected. The more you can associate the song with your specific source of irritation, the better. For example, earlier in the chapter, an individual used "These Are the Days," by 10,000 Maniacs, for two main reasons: (1) She loves the song and all the emotions it brings up in her that include how she and her partner have a deep and strong core relationship, and (2) she immediately associates the song with him and their first meeting.

   If your irritation on the way into work is, say, connected to your place of employment, maybe you can select a recording that you emotionally associate with work in a positive way. Put your playlist tracks together like that—by emotional association. Let's find a few recordings that can treat a variety of predictable sources of irritation that can affect you on your morning drive. That way when they arise, you will be ready.

   Music by artists like Jackson Browne, Bonnie Raitt, John Prine, Bob Dylan, the Grateful Dead, Green Day, and 10,000 Maniacs are great examples of music that not only calms your mood, but also focuses your attention.

   By musically rebalancing, you can prevent further frustration and get to work in a good mood, which can improve your overall performance and help you feel healthier mentally and physically.

2. **When You Miss Being Somewhere.** What if you're a little down because, for example, you miss being in the mountains and out in nature and were thinking about all the pleasurable trips you had made there in the past? Why not put on some nice music—let's say Mozart to stay calm and focused, or maybe a waltz by Chopin—to bring yourself into a more free-spirited frame of mind. Mix in some woodland scent that brings that environment to mind. Try closing your eyes and use some imagery—again, see yourself dancing, moving in a sunny meadow or other natural setting you remember from your past, when you really felt at ease. Now use those positive thoughts from the music and smells and your safe environment, and turn your thoughts into a real-life goal that will bring you a lot of pleasure. See yourself carving out a way to accomplish it. This will make you feel doubly good—first by thinking of something pleasurable, then by showing yourself a way to go out and get it for yourself.

Chapter 9

HOW TO USE MUSIC TO LIVE CREATIVELY

*Creative living is approaching life
awakened and conscious
of who we are, as well as maintaining a deep respect
and compassion for others. It is living completely
in the moment, happy and free.*

—Joseph Cardillo, from *Be Like Water*

Creative living is feeling alive and creating your own choices as you flow through life. When you live this way, you feel more balanced and blissful, less afraid of rejection, and more concerned about participating in life's endless creative possibilities presenting themselves from one moment to the next. You are more in favor with expressing who you really are rather than hiding it, and you wish others the same empowerment.

Up until now, we have been discussing how music can make your mind flow, keep it flowing, help you stay calm, focused, happy, and organized, improve your memory, strengthen your emotions, and tap the sound of your own brain waves. But once you bring all of these concepts to bear on the countless possibilities for living your life, the power of music becomes even greater. This is when your playlist can—and will, if you let it—launch you into a whole new level of living. Here, you will use your playlist to literally change your life. You will use it to give you the power to live each day creatively and to generate greater joy and success for yourself, your loved ones, and the world around you.

Living creatively, you will use your playlist to dissolve conflict and restriction whenever and wherever they appear in your life, and you will replace those feelings with happiness and freedom. Your life will become a work of art—a celebration of who you are, want to be, can be, and will be. Your inner desires and outer worlds become harmonious.

When you flow from this vantage point, you are most active, most natural; you nourish and you receive nourishment. You just keep following your bliss—to the point at which strength and healing become easier. At this level of your training, you are no longer "just" listening to various musical compositions that make you happy.

You have become the musical artist whose job it is to compose beauty in and through your life—so much of which you can change at will. And you will let your excitement for life and all of your creative possibilities come pouring out of you as you flow through each moment of living, creating the masterpiece that is you. And music, which has been embedded in you since your first cells began pulsating, will be there to help you every step of the way.

Keep Dreaming

By now, you know that many physical and psychological benefits arise in living from your most optimized mind-set. Your peak performance will increase in all that you do. And this will all lead to greater happiness and feelings of achievement and success. When your mind is flowing, your motivation, skill, and confidence are all high, and you feel you can rise to the occasion—whatever it is. In fact, you don't even think it; you just do it.

But it wasn't—and isn't—always this way. Just like the athlete trains to be in the zone, flow people have to train to keep flowing. Training your brain with music includes everything that we have discussed in this book so far. But there is one more component. Keep dreaming of new goals. And you will notice that, just like the athlete who plays in the zone makes superhuman plays look easy, you too will be better at accomplishing your dreams with much less effort, as long as you live from your best mind-set.

Just keep dreaming.

Dreams keep you from living a sedentary life. They help sustain flow and are a significant way to extend the flow mindset beyond the task of the moment.

Everyone experiences plateaus. When we do, many of us want to raise our bar of skills and achievements to get our energies flowing again. This is because when we are flowing, we feel most alive and creative. We are able to take in more of life's possibilities that are coming at us and coordinate our choices into other more positive life events that snowball into our future. We are happy and getting happier.

If we let life level out and stay that way, it is easy to feel like we have stopped growing. This can lead to feelings of boredom, low motivation, and lower self-esteem. It is hard to be creative when you feel this way, let alone to live creatively. However, as soon as we up the ante or the challenge, we often feel the buzz of excitement again. This comes from the anticipation of further accomplishments and the demand of mastering new skills to meet our challenges. All of a sudden, our world is less predictable. But it is more adventurous.

For people who live in flow, these scenarios are the absolute best. These become opportunities to grow, and to heighten your happiness and deepen your character.

Remember the dopamine connection. Your brain begins to release dopamine, bringing you pleasure, before you have even done anything—just from your anticipation of achievement.

The release of dopamine at the anticipation stage is significant. It is what makes animals hungry before they actually get food. It's what makes it so hard to pass a pizzeria and not buy a pizza. It's what helps you face challenges that will bring you closer to your dreams.

Research shows that the greater the demand or challenge an individual faces, the greater is the potential flow that the experience can launch. The opposite is also true: the lower the demand, the greater is the possibility of leveling off, getting bored, and falling out of flow. So it is important if you want to keep flowing—if you want to live your optimum—to keep your rewards coming and keep raising the bar.

When you feel that your life has leveled off or is headed

there, you can use music to take you to that peak of adventurous flow again. You can creatively start by using your favorite music to identify new dreams to move toward. One way you can do this is to put together a "Dream" playlist with tunes intended to help you: to free up your mind, to give you prompts, cues, hints, or partial solutions for how to raise the bar in your life. The following is a playlist you can check out from an individual who is familiar with our concepts. We encourage you, as always, to develop one based on your favorites and current goals. Notice how the tracks in this list arc from quicker rhythms with motivational lyrics to more relaxing music with less lyrical direction.

Sample "Dream" Playlist

▶ **"Free 2010,"** Ultra Nate (Bob Sinclair Remix DRM)

▶ **The Four Seasons,** Vivaldi

▶ **"The Climb,"** Miley Cyrus

▶ **"The Power of the Dream,"** Celine Dion

▶ **Adagio for Strings,** Samuel Barber

Find a quiet space. It doesn't matter if it is at home or at work, indoors or outdoors. It can be early morning, lunchtime, or at the end of the day. If you are tired during certain times, those would not be good times to induce a flow experience, and you may have to make other arrangements. Go to your quiet place daily. Spend some time, even a short time, there listening to your "Dream" playlist, and let the music guide you to getting in touch with your dreams. You may want to include some songs that have more aggressive and motivating lyrical and rhythmic content at the beginning to heighten your energy and to put you in the mood to break out of feeling plateaued.

Let yourself think about things you can strive for in your life that will make you happy. Ask yourself, "What would some of these things be?" Don't worry about how you would actually get them. Your job is just to make yourself aware of what those things are. For now, you can let the myriad images and ideas that emerge flow through your mind. Take your time with ones you like a lot. Think about why these things might be important to you. Think about whether they are challenging enough (but not too challenging) to give you that sense of adventure. You want to feel that you are raising the bar. Remember you are dreaming of things that will bring you to a better level of living. Stay focused as long as possible. These can be larger, longer-term goals or more immediate ones (ones you could attain today).

After a few days (or whatever time is necessary) pick a goal that keeps coming back to you in your reflections. Consider what new skills you will need to develop to meet the challenges presented by the dream.

For an example, imagine someone who has been teaching in elementary education for several years. When she goes to her quiet place, she dreams of writing a book about working with children. She is mostly happy at her teaching job and mostly happy with her life, but she feels that part of her is leveling off. Of course, she has situations at the school (like we all do at work) that are constantly presenting challenges and adventures, but these are not situations that she loves or looks forward to. They are more like annoyances. This is why such situations feel good only when they go away—or when the stressors they fuel go away.

Remember that things we love incite flow experiences. This is why you can use your dreams to launch such experiences.

For the teacher in our example, it is the dream of being an author that keeps coming back to her. Every time she sits quietly and listens to her peaceful music she sees herself: writing books, enjoying all the little things that doing so entails, giving talks about them to other people who also love education. She loves conversing. She thinks of writing as just another way to do that. And she loves to share ideas about education, so writing, she believes, can do that too. Even the thought of pursuing a second career in writing is exciting to her. She starts to feel a lot of pleasure just looking forward to the time she spends alone thinking about the possibility. It's time for her to take action.

Build Your Scaffolding

It is no secret that Albert Einstein loved music. In various writings and conversations, he referred to loving music so much that he could just as easily have become a musician. Perhaps that is why he saw much art in science and much science in art. Einstein's second wife, Elsa, gives us a glimpse at how he might have used music to build bridges in his own thinking process. "Music helps him," she once wrote, "when he is thinking about his theories. He goes to his study, comes back, strikes a few chords on the piano, jots something down, and returns to his study." To live creatively, we all often have to build temporary bridges to get from one place to another. They keep us flowing.

Music, just as Einstein used it, can help you build those bridges. And when you link bridges together toward a goal, we call this kind of bridge building SCAFFOLDING.

One of the important by-products of scaffolding is that it is capable of keeping you in a state of flow as you work out any chaos that emerges in your life from all the twists and turns you may encounter as you learn new skills toward fulfilling your dreams. It can do this because you are not asking yourself to take a huge leap into unknown territory, where you are not yet comfortable. You go there step by step. Let's think about our teacher. She may not have the skills to get what she wants yet. In her case, she works instead through her reflections to begin building a scaffold to get her there—she familiarizes herself with books on publishing, joins a writers' group, meets other educators who have written books on working with children, attends a writers conference, researches her manuscript, starts to put her book together, and so on.

So now her playlist is different. Rather than using mostly calming, peaceful music to help fuel her reflections, she uses music that works like think-aloud messages and cues to herself to get up and take the bull by the horns, so to speak. One of her favorite tracks is from the Rolling Stones, "You Can't Always Get What You Want." She loves and latches on to the lines, "But if you try sometime, you just might find / You get what you need." The following playlist is a sample of what she might listen to.

Sample "Go for It" Playlist

▸ **"You Can't Always Get What You Want,"** The Rolling Stones

....

▸ **"Turn the Beat Around,"** Gloria Estefan

....

▸ **"The Heat Is On,"** Glenn Frey

....

▸ **"It's My Life,"** Bon Jovi

....

▸ **"Soar,"** Christina Aguilera

....

Each of the songs on her playlist sends her direct instructions to go ahead, to get what she needs, and to get on task. Each energizes her in building the various steps in her scaffolding, and each motivates (and soothes) her through any anxieties she may feel from the turbulence of uncertainty that comes with change. This last point is worth emphasizing. Music not only helps you identify your dream and ease you as you build your scaffold but also comforts your anxieties as new challenges emerge. This helps you feel excitement rather than worry.

Scaffolding helps you see how several smaller, easily achievable tasks are linked to the major goal, and this fires up your brain's reward mechanism.

The more connection you see among the tasks, the more you can flow through them and among them—and the more you will be rewarded with pleasure along the way.

This feedback loop will exhilarate you at every juncture of your quest all the way to achieving your dream.

We know that specific mind-sets kick in when your brain sees a need for them—when they are advantageous. So essentially, you are training your brain to see challenges as adventures to flow in. As a result, you will experience your peak mind-set launching more automatically as you start to approach most of your day's challenges.

Playlist Bonus

Here is a chart to help you remember how music optimizes flow, sustains it, and helps you scaffold it outward—beyond individual tasks or goals—into all areas of life.

1. Music gets you into flow.
2. The flow mind-set can transfer to other things (especially with repetition).
3. You have to raise the bar (keep dreaming).
4. To stay in flow, you have to feel that you have the skills to meet the challenge or that you can acquire them (scaffold your goals).
5. Music balances you as the pendulum swings from challenge, to acquisition, to plateau, to challenge again.

> *Note:* Life is not stagnant, and neither are we. For this reason, we need to constantly adapt. This is why staying balanced is the core of this book.

Living creatively, we will make the world a better place. One of the greatest gifts we can return to the world is our fully developed dreams and our unique awareness. When we are flowing, it is easy to do good and to think positively and to fill the spaces we occupy with positive energy. Start and keep practicing these skills. Reap the rewards. Use your playlist to keep you positive. People look for places of harmony and balance for support in their own quests. You can be that support. Follow your happiness. It is natural. It is primal. It is you. Participate, compose, and be creative.

Putting Together Your Playlist

Here is how to begin choosing songs for a playlist that will help you live creatively.

- **First, pick songs you like a lot.**
- **Pay attention to when a certain song works and when it doesn't.**
- **Ingrain songs into your memory.**
- **Make a playlist that is task oriented. Train your brain with your assembled playlist.**
- **Look for new and old songs.**
- **Use guided imagery.**

> ▸ **Use a song's BPM to help you organize your playlist.**
>
> ▸ **Use your emotional connections to songs.**
>
> ▸ **Use your brain's reward system.**
>
> ▸ **Use songs you can empathize with.**
>
> ▸ **Use songs with useful metaphors.**
>
> ▸ **Use songs with strong and obvious rhythms.**
>
> ▸ **Attach your best memories to songs.**
>
> ▸ **Use songs to help you create.** Add calming, peaceful music to your playlist that can specifically help fuel your reflections. Also, try adding tracks that work like think-aloud messages and cues to yourself to get motivated and begin building the bridges to your dreams. Use these to help you stay flowing through the turbulence of change as you pursue your goals.

Exercise

1. **Create a Quiet Space.** Create a quiet space in your home where you can go for fifteen to thirty minutes a day. It doesn't have to be anything fancy. The idea is to make a place that offers you quiet and privacy. Put together a "Dream" playlist as described earlier in this chapter and play it. If such a space doesn't exist, try someplace outside your home, either outdoors or inside, that's welcoming and comfortable. The point is to get yourself away from all those things that require your attention during the day and allow you to shut the door on them for a while.

   Enter this space and be present to yourself. It may take a few minutes to quiet your thoughts. Notice the difference between thoughts of what others want from you and what you want. Make your thoughts about you.

2. **Reinvent Yourself.** Enter your quiet space. Play one, several, or all the tunes on your "Go for It" playlist. Pay special attention to the features of each tune that were responsible for you putting the song on the playlist. As you play the song(s), think about a larger-scale change you want to make in your life that would be in synch with one of the dreams you identified. But for now just think about that dream. For example, you may want to switch careers. What career appeals to you? What kind of employment would you like in that field? What major differences would you anticipate were you to enter that field? Financial? Social? Obligatory? Living? What qualifications are necessary? If you don't already have them, how can you get them? Ask yourself questions like these to see what it would practically take to reinvent this aspect of your life.

Contemplate yourself being in this position in five years (or whatever number is appropriate). Now break up the goal into smaller pieces and organize those into manageable components. Build your scaffolding from all these pieces so that it will get you to your goal. Focus on your plan. This may take you several sessions. Then move ahead.

Chapter 10

HOW TO USE YOUR BRAIN'S OWN MUSIC

"Your brain has its own signature as your fingerprints. It signs with your own music, your personalized soundtracks."

—Galina Mindlin

We've talked throughout this book about how your individual preferences greatly influence what music works the best for you. There is one way, however, to use the absolute best music for your brain to ensure you have the ultimate soundtrack that will fully optimize your own mind.

That soundtrack is music made from your own brain waves. This may sound strange, but it's real and it works. This music is known as BRAIN MUSIC THERAPY (BMT).

Lab experiments on BMT have shown that brain waves tend to reorganize themselves. When this happens, the brain waves are more responsive, and you can more accurately manipulate them, raising or lowering their frequencies as required. Therefore, music generated from your own brain waves allows you to experience longer-lasting, more sustainable effects than listening to other music.

In addition, extensive clinical experience shows that BMT is effective in helping you achieve alertness, calmness, improved organizational skills, emotional strength, improved mood, and sharpened memory. Many people have reported that they have been able to reduce and even completely eliminate their need for sleep and antianxiety medications as a result of BMT. We'll take a look at some of these effects of BMT later in the chapter.

The best part is that BMT, like all your playlist tunes, is noninvasive, has no negative side effects, and is enjoyable. It's much more cost effective than most medications. You can also use it just like you would any other playlist we have mentioned in this book. You can download it onto your iPod, with all your other playlists, and carry it right in your pocket with you wherever go, whenever you need it.

The Invention of BMT

Brain music therapy was developed in the early 1990s at the Moscow Medical Academy, in Russia, by Professor Dr. Yakov Levin, the same place where the iconic physiologist Dr. Ivan Pavlov launched the basics of neurophysiology. Following long-term efforts of a group of neurophysiologists, clinicians, and mathematicians led by Dr. Levin, a special technology was developed to turn a person's unique brain waves into piano music. This technology became known as BMT. The use of BMT as treatment for insomnia was first explored and studied by Dr. Levin in Russia, then expanded in Europe. It was then brought to the United States in 2005 by Dr. Mindlin, who had worked closely with Dr. Levin in Moscow.

Finding BMT

The main BMT center is located in New York City, but there are affiliate providers you can access across the country (for a list of providers, see the website Brain Music Therapy at www .brainmusictreatment.com). When you meet with a provider, he or she makes a five-minute recording of your EEG. First, the provider places a plastic cap, like a swimming cap, on your head. The cap holds the sensors that carry your EEG signals to a computer. Your EEG recording is then translated into personalized music tracks, with a special algorithm: one composition is for relaxing your brain, and another one is for activating it. The two pieces of music (your RELAXING FILE and your ACTIVATING FILE) are then converted into MP3 files. Once the conversion is complete (it generally takes three weeks as of this writing), you receive the music files on a CD.

The whole process is pretty laidback, and it takes only five minutes of sitting still and resting with your eyes closed to gather enough of your brain activity to create your individual brain musical scores.

For those who are not close to a provider, COMMON BMT FILES are in the making. These compositions are created from brain waves, but they are universal tracks, not ones customized to any particular individual. These files can also be found at the Brain Music Therapy website (www.brainmusictreatment.com). This means that if you want to add BMT tracks to your playlist, you can do that instantly by downloading the COMMON FILE, and if you want a customized recording of your individual brain waves, you can do that pretty quickly as well by visiting a provider near you.

When You Start Using BMT

When you start using BMT, you practice using your relaxing file and activating file (depending on which way you need to go) to keep you in your best balanced mind-set . You also want to listen to your relaxing file recordings every night before falling asleep and during the night anytime your sleep is interrupted. In the morning, you can listen to your activating file to get some instant energy. You can also listen to your BMT files as needed throughout the day for more alertness, to relax you, or to just balance yourself.

For example, you can use your BMT relaxing file to decrease feelings of being overwhelmed or anxious before heading into a contract negotiation, a classroom, meeting with your supervisor, or out on a date. To increase your focus or mental or physical energy, you can listen to your activating file.

But you can't expect to just turn on your CD and see immediate results as if you were popping a pill. To best train your brain, you need to listen to the files regularly over a period of several weeks, the same as any playlist track you are using to enhance your mind-set. In general, BMT users report positive results in three to four weeks. After that, positive results steadily increase until they reach full impact, which is usually somewhere around three months.

Sample BMT Playlist

▶ "BMT Activating File"

▶ "BMT Relaxing File"

Using BMT to Counter Insomnia

Many people have trouble falling asleep. Some of them have a ritual of reading a book or watching television until they eventually go down. And this works for them most of the time. Many less fortunate individuals have to deal with bouts of sleepless nights. Some people have another sort of sleep problem. Getting to sleep is no issue, but then they wake up unfailingly in the middle of the night, every single night, and stare at the ceiling wide awake. Others get up to go to the bathroom or to get a drink of water and then find it impossible to get back to sleep.

Thoughts start racing through their heads. Sometimes they start rehashing the day at work, what went right, wrong, or what didn't go at all. Some people's minds take them on a journey of interpersonal hassles. Some just give up trying to sleep, go to their computer, try not to wake the family, and do some work or browse the Internet. By 5:00 a.m. or 5:30 a.m., they get tired of that and go to bed for only an hour or two before their alarm starts screaming at them. They drag themselves to work so exhausted at the beginning of the day that they feel as if they've already worked a whole week.

One such individual recently brought himself to the BMT

center, skeptical but feeling there wasn't much to lose. When he finally used his BMT relaxing track, he wasn't surprised. His eyes remained wide open, and sleep seemed as distant as usual. It was 2:30 a.m., and his brain was running circles, right on schedule.

He had an issue with the music. He didn't like it. It is not that he minded it completely, but it definitely was not the kind of music he would have chosen to listen to in his leisure time. But he really wanted to give it a chance—he'd tried so many other things. His doctor informed him that his insomnia had taken a long time to get to where it was as a condition; he shouldn't expect it to just go away in a few minutes. So he already knew that one play wasn't going to do it. He ended up playing the song four or five times before he felt anything. And in the end, he did feel a little better—his mind became less active. The next thing he knew, he was waking up to his alarm, and it was the next morning. So he'd managed to get to sleep and make it through the night. But he really didn't feel that much different for the first three or four days.

He continued training. As the days went by, little by little, he started feeling a difference. The biggest difference was that his wake-up time in the middle of the night started getting shorter and shorter. He eventually stopped getting up for night dates with his computer and would dive into his relaxing file instead, which took him deeper and deeper into sleep. His sleeping got better, and in about six weeks, he could admit that nighttime awakenings had shortened significantly. To his surprise, he even had occasions when he was sleeping through the whole night. Of course, he still has nights from time to time when he has to listen to his relaxing file many times, but those nights come less frequently and are replaced mostly by good nights of restful sleeping.

In the morning, he listens to his activating file and then heads out to work with much less—if any—stress. On his way to work he listens to his "Driving to Work" playlist:

Sample "Driving to Work" Playlist

▸ **"Mrs. Robinson,"** Simon and Garfunkel (on *The Concert in Central Park*)

▸ **"She May Call You Up Tonight,"** Left Banke

▸ **"I Wanna Be a Lifeguard,"** Blotto

▸ **"Take It Easy,"** Eagles

▸ **"I Can See for Miles,"** The Who

He finds that listening to his BMT activating file beforehand has intensified the flow effect of his "Driving to Work" tracks and that it lasts longer into the day.

Another individual who used to feel like her head was spinning all day long—in charge of so many operations, people, and projects—also had trouble getting to sleep at night. In addition to that, she had difficulty waking up in the morning. She would go to work feeling like that old Pete Seeger song,

"My Get Up and Go Has Got Up And Went." Her lack of gusto would continue all day.

But then when she'd go back home in the evening, she'd feel restless again and resort to watching television after dinner until around midnight. Her jumpy mind-set was so strong that it would irritate her dog until he'd start pacing around the apartment until all hours of the night. When she was unable to control things, she'd resort to popping some AMBIEN or drinking a few glasses of wine or something stronger, especially when things at work weren't going that great. Then she'd be up and out of the apartment at 6 a.m. again, at which time she'd pump herself up with three cups of strong coffee in the first coffee shop that opened in her neighborhood.

For her, the BMT relaxing file was the perfect medicine to

▸▸ I use my BMT relaxing file when I plan on jogging at the end of a long day. This is because, for me, I tend to still be in teaching or research mode for a while after work unless I consciously try to cut down the time it takes me to naturally make the transition into a lighter mind-set. On most days when I jog, I am trying for about five miles, and I want to be as fluid as possible, mentally and physically. I find that playing a BMT relaxing track first, then as I am getting into my jogging gear, putting on the activating file, I get the fluidity I am looking for. Then when I actually hit the road, I put on my regular "Jogging" playlist. When I do this, I find that I reap more benefit from all of the various tunes. The effects are stronger, last longer, and I perform better. This intensifies my happiness and flow.

—Joseph

get her to sleep at night. Like most people who use BMT, it took a while before she really felt its full effects, but once she did, it worked faster than a drug. Sometimes she would wake up in the middle of the night and just hear the song in her head and—zap!—she was out.

She used her BMT activating file in the morning, which allowed her to eliminate two of her usual three cups of coffee in just a few weeks. One time, she forgot her iPod at home, so she couldn't listen to her activating file. But soon enough, she started hearing her activating file playing from memory in her mind—and it worked automatically, just as her nighttime track worked automatically. Next thing she knew, she felt alert.

And this is it. This is what you want to happen. Once you've entrained your brain, any of the songs on your playlist will eventually start going off automatically in your head, preparing your mind and body for the desired effect you want and when you want it.

This is exactly what you are going for in training your brain to respond to specific situations with music.

Bye-Bye, Anxiety

You can also use your relaxing track to help you get rid of anxiety. When using BMT, both in studies as well as in clinical settings around and outside the United States, patients with anxiety (generalized anxiety disorder) report significant decreases in their condition in about 80 percent of cases. Similarly, many patients with panic disorders report being free of attacks after using BMT. Patients with social phobia who use a relaxing BMT file for fifteen to twenty minutes before public speaking have reported feeling significantly less worried while on stage. And for anyone trying to reduce medications taken for anxiety, more than half the patients with insomnia and anxiety have been able to decrease the initial dosage of their medications, and quite a few patients were able to use BMT as their main treatment.

One individual who'd had enough of having to deal with anxiety attacks said that, for him, the attacks would come as they pleased, uninvited, and especially at times he least expected them. One in particular was very embarrassing to him because he was sitting with his friends in a park after a movie and started feeling his heart beating faster and faster. He tried gasping for air but couldn't catch his breath. Then he heard his friends shouting: "What's going on? You look terrified!"

He was not OK. He had been going to therapy, and he took medications. And still he was vulnerable and embarrassed by these events because they continued.

It took a good month of using his BMT files daily, but he eventually started experiencing fewer attacks, which were a lot less intense when they came. In fact, his episodes dropped from seven to ten a month to just a few.

Other individuals have reported similar successes, especially in areas such as public speaking, stage fright, and even fear of flying.

The Happiness in Your Pocket

Like other songs on your playlist, BMT will also work to regulate mood swings or depression, only with more strength, precision, and staying power. For example, listening to a BMT activating file every morning and during the times of day when you might feel withdrawn, unmotivated, and otherwise depressed will significantly shift your moods into something more positive.

One individual who suffered from depression said she would wake up in the morning, wishing she could just stay in bed with her eyes closed all day. It wasn't because she was tired—more because she was feeling so down. She described herself as feeling sad all day long for no reason at all. She even stopped doing some of the usual things that would snap her out of her depression, like hanging out with her friends, having fun with her boyfriend, even playing with her pet cat. She started taking medications, which improved her mood. But waking up in the morning was still very, very difficult. It was not waking up itself, she said, but the gloomy thoughts that would follow. This routine complicated other things too, making her late for work and stressing out her relationship with her boss. Although her boss was very understanding, she was still her boss and expected a certain quality of performance. She was on two antidepressants already, but those gloomy hours in the morning were still hard for her to shake off.

When she started using a BMT activating file, the first thing she noticed was that she was taking much less time to get prepared for work. By the end of three weeks, she actually started feeling happier in the morning. She could get herself out of bed much more easily and get herself to work feeling content. She has learned to use the BMT activating file during the middle of her day now as well to pump up her energy (and mood) when it starts to go down.

Again, any of your relaxing or activating tracks on your playlist will have a similar effect, although not as dramatic as those coming from your own customized BMT recording.

Playlist Bonus

You may want to play your BMT first, optimize your mind-set, and further enhance it with tracks for specific playlists. For example, you can combine BMT with an earlier sample playlist for alertness. This turns your iPod or MP3 player into an ultimate pocket-size mind enhancer.

Sample "Alertness" Playlist (Showing BMT Inclusion Track)

▸ "BMT Activating File"

▸ **"Whole Lotta Love,"** Led Zeppelin

▸ **"Walk This Way,"** Aerosmith

▸ **"Any Way You Want It,"** Journey

▸ **"We're An American Band,"** Grand Funk Railroad

BMT Battles ADHD

People with attention-deficit/hyperactivity disorder (ADHD) who use BMT generally listen to their BMT activating file early in the morning and then again around noon. These are times when they would typically take a dosage of prescribed stimulants. Using music, however, is a lot more fun and without the risk of negative side effects. In addition, ADHD individuals often listen to their activating file fifteen to twenty minutes at various times throughout their daily routines, especially before doing something that requires greater focus. This practice gets them flowing and keeps them focused and engaged.

However, using BMT as a treatment for ADHD is not an overnight cure—BMT doesn't work that way. Most people with ADHD report that their concentration and performance increase within two to three months of regularly listening to their BMT files. Some have been able to reduce the dosage of their medications under physician supervision, and some have used BMT as stand-alone treatment.

Bye-Bye, Headaches; Hello, Good Vibrations

What if you get headaches? Research has shown very good results in using BMT to treat both tension and migraine headaches. Clinical reports show that after regularly listening to BMT files, patients commonly report overall decreases in the frequency and intensity of headaches. The aura phase—when people feel that the headache is coming on—is when you typically feel dizzy, heavy, or weak, and your blood pressure may drop. It is at this point that you can keep the headache at bay by listening to your BMT activating file to invigorate you. If, however, a migraine persists, you can move on to your relaxing file. This will wind you down as well as decrease the intensity and length of the headache.

Here is a common scenario and outcome using BMT. One individual we know tried using his BMT files to treat what he described as "killer" headaches. They would come whenever a stressful situation occurred, the weather changed, and sometimes out of nowhere. This headache's M.O. was that it would come on gradually and make him feel very weak, tired, dizzy, and sort of heavy. He found that listening to an activating BMT track from his playlist would ward off the headache most of the time. But if he couldn't shut it down right away, he found he could put on his relaxing file and just keep that on for the whole time during the attack. For him, this approach has made his headaches much less intense and less frequent.

BMT Music in the Real World

When you think of the term *first responder*, what may come to mind are thoughts of responsibility, stress, and long hours of little or no sleep. First responders are a wide variety of people: law enforcement officers, firefighters and medical techs, doctors and nurses, the people running our safety infrastructure. The men and women working these jobs need to be mentally and physically ready for anything that may come their way, often unexpectedly. And this can be challenging. Sometimes these individuals meet their challenges by relying on things like coffee, tea, and supplements to help them stay alert and flowing.

The biggest liability for first responders is lack of sleep. Add to this a pattern of poor eating habits, and you have a combustible combination. When sleep and diet are not managed correctly, they can have a major impact on anyone's job performance and overall life satisfaction. So a nonmedicinal, no-side-effects sleep aid for first responders is often a welcome addition to their daily health and wellness—as is a functional nutrition program, using the right food at the right time for the right task, so they can attempt to adjust their eating habits on and off the job.

For these reasons, DuRousseau's company, Human Bionics, received research support from the Department of Homeland Security to put together a study to find out whether BMT was effective at improving sleep and other measures of general wellness for forty-one law enforcement officers and firefighters who participated in an eight-week study. This WELLNESS STUDY was a necessary first step in validating alternative approaches to the use of medications as the only viable intervention for improving sleep quality, mood, and job performance in real-life situations.

The idea was to give each person in the test group his or her own relaxing and activating BMT files. They used an MP3 player on their phones to listen to the tracks when working in the field, at the office, or at home. They also filled out a 128-question survey on several occasions to track changes in their behavior over the course of the study. Their answers to the questions were intended to measure any improvements they experienced in sleep, mood, and life satisfaction.

In an article recently published about the BMT results from the Wellness Study, DuRousseau and Mindlin found that BMT made a difference. After four weeks of using their relaxing and activating files, the test group reported significant changes in sleep quality, insomnia, depression, and job performance. A separate control group did not receive their own brain music for this study; instead, they were given compositions made from someone else's brain waves. Keeping the testing as accurate as possible and adding some intrigue on the side, subjects didn't know which group they were in (whether they had their own or someone else's brain waves on file). On all the assessments, the test subjects with their own BMT music reported experiencing greater improvements in sleep, mood, and performance than those in the control group.

These results extend the scope of earlier clinical insomnia research by Dr. Mindlin and colleagues, finding similar outcomes to the laboratory results, yet expanding the study into a real-world, normal working and living environment. For the first time, a music-based neurotraining (NT) intervention had been scientifically evaluated (among a population of on-the-job first responders) and was found to improve sleep, reduce anxiety and stress, and improve job performance without the need for potentially harmful drugs.

What We've Learned

We have come a long way in the field of neuroscience over the past two decades. Clinical trials and a real-world study have demonstrated that BMT is effective at reducing stress and anxiety, improving symptoms of insomnia and depression, and improving on-the-job performance. Today, we have brain-sensing devices and computers at our fingertips—we can instantly make customized music files, download them, and use them to influence our brain and guide our moods and motivations in one direction or another. At the time this book went to press, the entire BMT procedure cost $550, but innovations mean that lower costs, additional providers, and a faster turnaround time (one hour) are expected soon.

This great potential in the field of mental health is almost scary, but also very fascinating. We have seen only the tip of the iceberg in terms of the potential uses of neurotechnology, and we will see many amazing new brain-interfacing products coming down the pipeline over the next decade or two. It is important to remember that the field of EEG neuroimaging has evolved to the point where we can tell that a specific brain activity pattern is consistent with a certain neuropsychiatric disorder. We can also tell whether there is a particular pattern of brain activity that marks your peak level of performance. Soon, there will be products and service companies that will take advantage of these notions and move into what many will see as the next generation of music and the mind.

Your playlist could be a new beginning, that revolutionary first step toward a symphony of peace, emotional balance, and creativity.

Putting Together Your Playlist

› First, pick songs you like a lot.

› Pay attention to when a certain song works and when it doesn't.

› Ingrain songs into your memory.

› Make a playlist that is task oriented. Train your brain with your assembled playlist.

› Look for new and old songs.

› Use guided imagery.

› Use a song's BPM to help you organize your playlist.

› Use your emotional connections to songs.

› Use your brain's reward system.

› Use songs you can empathize with.

› Use songs with useful metaphors.

› Use songs with strong and obvious rhythms.

› Attach your best memories to songs.

› Use songs that help you create.

› Add BMT files to your playlist.

CONCLUSION

Through harmony all things are influenced.

—Confucius

The fact that music connects us to the vibrant power of our body's cell-by-cell creation and to the vibrational power of all things in the universe, as well as to the universe itself, makes its influence on us—and on all life—worthy of our attention. Powerful and measurable as many of its effects can be, however, music cannot take away life's challenges. But music *can* change the way we respond to them.

Your attraction to specific music and the effects it has on you are as unique as your own fingerprints. As such, we have discussed a set of practical tools that will enable you to scientifically identify the unique way your individual body and mind respond to music and the many options those responses give you. The more you practice and experiment with the techniques and concepts, the more effectively you will be able to sharpen your personal playlists to meet your distinct life challenges and goals. We believe this is a path charged with choice, skill, courage, love, and self-empowerment. It is a simple and enjoyable way to end old, dysfunctional patholo-gies and replace them with new feelings and new actions that will optimize your mind-set—whatever your goal.

Keep your personal playlist in your pocket or briefcase, in your car, home, or office, and it will be there to help you stay calm and focused and perform at your best, wherever you are. Use it to help you fight insomnia, anxieties, stress, fears; to improve your mood; and to keep your emotions in check. There is a saying in Zen Buddhism: "Flow with whatever may happen; let your mind be free. Hold close to center. Stay balanced. This is the ultimate." It is our hope that the skills discussed in this book will bring you closer to center and help make your life journey more enjoyable and creative by help-ing you balance and harmonize in all the environments you may enter.

May you find peace and beauty and healing by using your own vibrations, rhythms, and brain waves to resonate, as a par-ticle of the universe, within yourself and then within the rest of the world.

And when every brain regains its plasticity, every society will become healthier, and the world will become more har-monious. Be well.

GLOSSARY

ACTIVATING FILE: One of two musical compositions created during the Brain Music Therapy process that is intended to provide an instant pick-me-up in arousal and concentration levels.

ACTIVELY LISTENING: Paying closer attention to how the music you are listening to is being made and the effects it has on you.

ALPHA: Brain waves that engender a state of mind associated with relaxed-alert.

AMBIEN: A prescription medication used for the short-term treatment of insomnia.

AREA 19: One of fifty-two distinct brain areas. Area 19 is your brain's visual processing center.

AREA 22: One of fifty-two distinct brain areas. Area 22 is located near the temporal lobe and is where you begin your process of reading musical notes and associating them with actually playing the notes or hearing them played on a musical instrument as well as enjoying them as music.

BETA: Brain waves that engender a state of mind associated with your waking state, in which you feel most alert.

BAP: Refers to brain activity pattern.

BRAIN ACTIVITY PATTERN (BAP): As measured by an EEG device, is a person's unique pattern of brain wave activity collected during resting eyes-open and eyes-closed periods. A person's BAP is stable over time and can be compared to a group BAP to determine where imbalances exist in the brain wave activity.

BPM: Beats per minute in a song.

BMT: Brain Music Therapy.

BRAIN MUSIC THERAPY: A patented treatment for insomnia and mood-related problems that creates two individualized music compositions from the listener's brain waves; one for relaxing and the other for activating the brain's key systems.

BWP: Brain-wave pattern.

CENTRAL EXECUTIVE: This term is used by psychologists and neuroscientists to describe a loosely defined collection of brain processes that are responsible for planning, cognitive flexibility, abstract thinking, rule acquisition, making appropriate actions, and inhibiting inappropriate ones.

COGNITIVE NEUROSCIENCE: The study of how thought processes take place in the human brain to understand the specific psychological steps that are required to perform any particular task or set of tasks.

COMMON BMT FILE: BMT files created to match brain waves, but a universal track, not one customized to any one particular individual.

COMMON FILES: Refers to universal BMT files.

CROSS-FREQUENCY PHASE COUPLING: The process by which the

brain communicates between nearby and distinct neural systems to coordinate the mental activities needed to accomplish a particular task.

DELTA: Brain waves that engender a state of mind in which deep sleep occurs. This state is also associated with trances.

DEFAULT MODE: The default mode network is an interconnected and anatomically defined system active when the brain is at rest. It preferentially activates when you focus on internal tasks like daydreaming, thinking about the future, retrieving memories, and gauging others' perspectives.

DISSONANCE: Pleasant-sounding chords and intervals are referred to as consonance, whereas unpleasing ones are referred to as dissonance. Musical harmonies or beats that seem distant or slightly incomplete and which your mind wants to correct or resolve.

DOPAMINE: A neurotransmitter formed in the brain and associated with reward-seeking behaviors.

EEG: Electroencephalogram or electroencephalograph. The measure of electrical activity generated by the brain, picked up by sensors on the scalp. EEG waves are summed voltage fluctuations resulting from ionic current flows within the neurons of the brain. In clinical contexts, EEG refers to the recording of the brain's spontaneous electrical activity over a short period of time, usually 20–40 minutes, as recorded from multiple electrodes placed on the scalp.

ELECTROENCEPHALOGRAM: A graphic record of the electrical activity of the brain as recorded by an electroencephalograph.

ELECTROENCEPHALOGRAPH: The device used to measure and/or record brain waves.

EMPATHY: Ability to understand another person's feelings.

ENTRAINING: When brain rhythms in one system speed up or slow down to match a stronger external rhythm, perhaps being generated by a different neural system as a means to coordinate activity.

EPINEPHRINE: Also called adrenaline. A hormone secreted by the adrenal glands that is released into the bloodstream in response to physical or mental stress in order to initiate many bodily responses, including the stimulation of heart rate and increased blood pressure and blood glucose concentration.

FIRST RESPONDER: An occupation that relates to the protection and/or emergency medical care of others and typically includes law enforcement, firefighters, emergency medical staffs, and other frontline forces intended to prevent terrorist acts and assist injured persons.

FLOW: A state of concentration so focused that it amounts to absolute absorption in an activity.

FLOWING: In a flow state.

HARMONY: A parallel melody or cluster of notes played or sung simultaneously to the original or main melody.

MOTHERESE: The sing-song ways that parents speak to their children before and after birth.

NEUROPHYSIOLOGY: The study of the functional processes of the brain and nervous system related to normal and abnormal development and behavior.

NEUROPSYCHIATRY: The use of human neuroanatomy and neurophysiology in the diagnoses and treatment of mental imbalances associated with a wide range of psychological and psychiatric illnesses.

NOREPINEPHRINE: A hormone and a neurotransmitter that plays a role in mood enhancement, as well as things like increased alertness and motivation.

NORMAL (BRAIN RHYTHMS): A combination of brain wave oscillations from near zero to over 100 Hertz (oscillations per second) with a normal distribution of system-wide brain activity patterns during resting and active cognitive states. Brain rhythms are named for their frequency ranges, where Delta = 1–4 Hz, Theta = 5–8 Hz, Alpha = 9–12 Hz, Beta = 13–30 Hz, and Gamma is more than 30 Hz.

NOT NORMAL (BRAIN RHYTHMS): A statistically significant difference in amplitude and/or frequency measures of an individual's brain waves as determined by an age-matched quantitative EEG normative database, as well as with functional testing and clinical observation.

NT: Neurotraining.

PLASTICITY: The brain's ability to change at any age.

PLEASURE PRINCIPLE: Term coined by Freud in 1911, referring to people's tendency to seek pleasure and avoid pain.

RELAXING FILE: One of two musical compositions created during the Brain Music Therapy process that is intended to provide an instant reduction in arousal level and insomnia symptoms.

RESONANCE: The duration of a note, its reverberation.

RHYTHM: A pattern or recurrence of beat.

SALIENCE NETWORK: One of the three main systems of the brain. The Salience Network (SN) is the system responsible for things like empathy, social behaviors, and making changes to your actions.

SCAFFOLDING: When you link smaller goals together toward a larger goal.

SEROTONIN: Sometimes called the happy hormone because of its contributions to sleep and good moods.

SKINNER BOX: A box in which an animal (particularly a rat) can be placed to study its behavior. It contains a lever the animal can move to receive a reward (food) or punishment (electric shock). Named after the American psychologist B. F. Skinner (1904–1990).

SUB-NETWORKS: The systems in the brain responsible for processing a particular input and responding with a specific pattern of activity, like seeing and hearing. Other sub-networks can be responsible for fight or flight, pleasure or pain, and even addictive behaviors. Sub-networks are typically connected through feedback loops to the key brain control networks as well as to each other.

SYNAPSE: A synapse is the location of intercellular communication between nerve cells. Synapses are typically associated with two cells: the presynaptic neuron and the postsynaptic neuron. The presynaptic neuron is the cell that sends the message (using neurotransmitters), while the postsynaptic neuron is the cell that receives the message and acts upon it.

SYNCHRONY: Refers to all of the parts included within a musical composition staying on beat or in step, and it typically requires a leader or conductor to keep all parts working together. In the brain, the frontal cortex, which monitors all of its activity, sends directions back through connections in both halves of the brain to keep everything coordinated.

THETA: Associated with deeper relaxation. The state of mind you feel between wakefulness and sleep. Theta is sometimes referred to as "dreamer's brain."

WELLNESS STUDY: A cross-over controlled evaluation of music-based neurofeedback training as a means to improve sleep and job performance of forty-one law enforcement officers and firefighters in the Metro-Washington, D.C. area.

INDEX

ABOUT THE AUTHORS

Photo Credit: Shawn Allie

Galina Mindlin, MD, PhD, is an assistant clinical professor of psychiatry at Columbia University, College of Physicians and Surgeons, and is the supervising attending physician in the Department of Psychiatry and Behavioral Health at St. Luke's Roosevelt Hospital Center. She is board certified in psychiatry and neurology and holds a PhD in neuro-physiology and neuropsychology.

Dr. Mindlin is a founder of Brain Music Therapy (BMT) in the United States. In addition, she is clinical director and executive director of the BMT Center in New York, works with twenty BMT providers across the United States, and is in private practice in New York City. She has published articles, made numerous presentations at scientific conferences, and is currently a lead investigator on BMT for insomnia and anxiety and co-investigator on BMT in first responders. Dr. Mindlin is a Chief Medical Officer for HaPI

(Health Performance International), one of the Founders of MindFitness International, and Medical Director at Peak NT. Along with her colleagues, she is on a mission to bring evidence-based wellness MindFitness programs to people to help them stay mentally sharp; to increase their peak performance; and to fight stress, insomnia, addiction, and anxiety. She is active in teaching residents, students, and interns.

For the past several years, Dr. Mindlin gave more than eighty interviews on BMT technology, including with *O Magazine*, the *New York Post*, *Barron's*, *Gotham*, *Vogue*, *USA Today*, and *Time Out*. She has also been featured on *Good Morning America*, *The Today Show*, Fox News, ABC, MSNBC, CBS, NY1, and Reuters, and she has made many other television appearances.

Photo Credit: Bob Health

Don DuRousseau, MBA, is a cognitive neuroscientist. He is the founder and chief executive officer of Human Bionics, LLC, and executive director of Peak Neurotraining Solutions, Inc. He has more than twenty years of scientific, clinical, and business experience in brain measurement systems and neurofeedback training technologies. He is an internationally recognized neuroscientist, electroencephalogram (EEG) system developer, entrepreneur, and neuroethicist whose specialization is mathematical methods and systems for analyzing the electrical activity of the brain and body. DuRousseau has held senior management positions in the neurodiagnostic industry, where he was extensively involved in the development of leading-edge EEG and epilepsy source localization systems, integrated EEG and functional MRI acquisition devices, and transcranial Doppler technologies. His present research interests lie in standardizing the applications and use of quantitative EEG and neurotraining services and promoting their ethical use in clinical and real-world environments. He has been the principal investigator on several neurotechnology research-and-development grants and contracts from Defense Advanced Research Projects Agency, National Institutes of Health, Virginia Center for Innovative Technology, and Department of Homeland Security, and is an invited grant reviewer for the National Institutes of Health for applications in neuroimaging, neuroprosthetic, and implantable brain-computer interface applications. He holds four patents and is the author of more than a dozen peer-reviewed journal articles and reports on neuroethics and neurotechnology developments. He is active as a board member, mentor, and speaker for several community and university neuroscience programs. Don graduated with a degree in neurobiology from University of California-Berkeley and has an MBA in international business and public policy from George Washington University.

Photo Credit: E. Cardillo

Joseph Cardillo, PhD, is a top-selling author in the fields of health, mind-body-spirit, and psychology. His books *Can I Have Your Attention?— How to Think Fast, Find Your Focus, and Sharpen Your Concentration; Be Like Water;* and *Bow to Life* have inspired people of all ages and backgrounds worldwide. Foreign-language editions of his work have appeared in German, Russian, Portuguese, Arabic, Korean, Malaysian, Chinese, and Indian. As an educator, he has taught more than twenty thousand students at several universities, including the University at Albany-SUNY and Hudson Valley Community College, where he is a professor of English and creative writing. He is a research associate at Mind-Body Medical University and has a doctorate in holistic psychology and mind-body medicine. Dr. Cardillo is a contributor to the Great Parenting Academy and writes a popular blog on attention training for *Psychology Today*. He received the prestigious 2011 State University of New York Chancellor's Award for Scholarly Research.

He regularly teaches workshops in health and wellness at various colleges and institutions. Dr. Cardillo is also active in clinical research, programming and development, and group consultation in the Whole Person Health and Education Program, which includes physical, emotional, cognitive, social, and cultural wellness, at the Mind-Body Health Foundation and Mind-Body Medical University Clinics, South Pasadena,

California. He specializes in corporate, educational, athletic, and professional group consultation.

He is a black-belt martial arts specialist and master of five martial arts.

Author websites

Galina Mindlin: Brain Music Therapy,
 www.brainmusictreatment.com

Don DuRousseau: PEAK Neurotraining Solutions,
 www.peaknt.com

Joseph Cardillo: www.josephcardillo.com

Your Playlist Can Change Your Life: http://yourplaylist.co

My Playlists

- ▶
- ▶
- ▶
- ▶
- ▶
- ▶
- ▶
- ▶
- ▶
- ▶
- ▶
- ▶
- ▶

My Playlists

▶

▶

▶

▶

▶

▶

▶

▶

▶

▶

▶

▶

▶

My Playlists

▶

▶

▶

▶

▶

▶

▶

▶

▶

▶

▶

▶

▶

▶

My Playlists

▶

▶

▶

▶

▶

▶

▶

▶

▶

▶

▶

▶

▶

My Playlists

▶

▶

▶

▶

▶

▶

▶

▶

▶

▶

▶

▶

▶

My Playlists

▶

▶

▶

▶

▶

▶

▶

▶

▶

▶

▶

▶

▶

▶

My Playlists

▶

▶

▶

▶

▶

▶

▶

▶

▶

▶

▶

▶

▶